CONTENTS

Foreword	0
Energisers ~ The Cup that Cheers	1
Soups	2
Salads in Gravies	3
Salad Bar ~ Crunches and Curls	4
Veggie Bazaar ~ How Green is My Valley and Red and Purple	5
Rice is Nice	6
Bread Basket	7
Tea with Me	8
Dip, Dip, Dip ~ Chutneys, Raitas and Sauces	9
Dals and Other Accompaniments	10
One-Dish Meals	11
Sinless Sweets ~ Well Almost	12
Spice-It-Up Masalas	13
Tips for a Healthier Lifestyle	14

FOREWORD

Understanding your enemy is important. In the case of health – the enemy comes in many avatars – aggressive fats and cholesterol, truant insulin, hyperactive bile, see-sawing blood pressure, so on and so forth. About 10 years ago I first acknowledged these common enemies. Hence this aspiration to a life well lived. Hippocrates' trusim, 'You are what you eat', never sounded truer than in modern times. In our race to make a product commercially viable we change it so radically that the goodness quotient is the first to get thrown out of the kitchen window. Ingredients get processed, refined and modified to suit our so-called aesthetic demands of sight, smell and taste. And yet not one among us can deny that some of our earliest and most happy memories are linked inextricably to the aroma and taste of honest-to-goodness home cooked comfort food.

And so I embarked on this journey of rediscovery of energising foods. It helped of course that I had parents to whom eating right was a lifestyle, not a passing fad. Gradually, I tried, one ingredient in one dish at a time, to modify our hybridised meals, to up the goodness quotient. I can't say that the family cheered me on endlessly. Far from it – there were times when on the spot renaming of ingredients had to be done if they had already suffered a bad reputation. At other times the folks were totally puzzled, albeit pleasantly, by the elaborate presentation of a dish, guessing that it camouflaged some ulterior motive. But they went through it all sportingly, hoping that either good sense or good taste might emerge one day.

Meanwhile the results of these experiments had begun to be seen. The kids were fast outgrowing their chronic bouts of cough and cold, and we were all looking trimmer and feeling fitter. Shedding weight had not been one of the main objectives but increasing energy levels had definitely been one. Let me caution that I am no nutritionist. But a lifetime, or what seems like one, of editing health, fitness and cookery pages, gave me some valuable insights into how the body and mind react and interact with the various foods we indulge ourselves with. And also the fact that there were alternatives available. Many of the recipes actually took the best from the past and added onto it, which again brought home the realisation that mother always knew best. And I sincerely hope that will ring true of future generations too. Fat hope or slim chance, the choice is yours to make. Make it now!

HEALTHY COOKING

MORE THAN
100 SMART
WAYS TO
GOOD
HEALTH

Sandhya Rajayer

Zaika

Zaika is an imprint of
BPI (INDIA) PVT LTD
ISBN 81-7693-022-9
© Sandhya Rajayer, 2002
Photography: Arvind Sawant

Published by
Zaika

Block No. 50, Evergreen Ind. Est,
Shakti Mills Lane, Off Hains Road,
Mahalaxmi, Mumbai - 400 011.
Tel : 492 1737/492 1906 Fax: 492 2538
E-mail: bpipl@vsnl.com / bpibooks@vsnl.net
All rights reserved

ENERGISERS ~ THE CUP THAT CHEERS

Which comes first – the wake up aroma of the morning brew or the wake up itself? It's the eternal chestnut – the chicken or the egg? But tea is not just the name of the brown concoction as we know it. Tea is actually a decoction of any substance usually brewed and consumed hot. There are also a variety of green teas which are infusions (that is boiling hot water is poured on the green tea leaves). But here I am speaking of health-giving herbal teas. My introduction to them happened when my parents moved to the south Indian city of Mysore.

A city of palaces and gardens, it also has customs that are peculiar to the populace. When my mother and I went visiting we were offered the customary tea. My mother, who doesn't know the taste of tea to this day, happily accepted, to my consternation.

It turned out to be lemon grass tea. The most instantly invigorating drink I've had. Apparently, our folk make an art of combining caring and hospitality. You'll find a dozen types of herbal teas here. Some are need-based, others can be enjoyed for their rejuvenating qualities. And yes, they are all teas.

Makes 3 cups

Lemon Grass Tea

Lemon grass tea is great to drain away the congestion in the respiratory tract. That is perhaps the first remedy for the common cold or cough that mothers in rural India think of. But you could have it any time you feel like a hot cuppa, but of course, as in everything else, have it in moderation.

Ingredients

Chopped lemon grass, fresh/dried	1 cup
Cardamom, crushed	2
Cloves	3
Fresh ginger	2 inch piece
Or dried ginger powder	1 tsp
Fresh turmeric root	1 inch piece
Or turmeric powder	1 tsp
Coriander seeds	1 tsp
Cumin seeds	1 tsp
Ajwain	¼ tsp
Black pepper corns	¼ tsp
Jaggery	to taste

Method

Put all these ingredients, except the jaggery, in 6 cups of water and boil till reduced to half the quantity. After it comes to a boil let the tea simmer, do not cook on a high flame. This is best for infusing the essences of the various ingredients. Add the jaggery and take off flame. Ideally you should have this fresh but for purposes of convenience you can store the decoction in the refrigerator and reheat before consuming the next day.

Makes 1 cup

Garlic Tea

The unpleasant odour of garlic is due to its sulphur content, which is what also gives it antiseptic properties. Garlic dissolves mucus in the sinuses. It is also effective in combating high blood pressure by easing the spasm of the small arteries.

Ingredients

Pepper	1½ tsp
Garlic	10 cloves
Onion, chopped	1
Ginger, chopped	1½ inch piece
Sliced jaggery	1 cup
Turmeric powder	1 tsp
Cloves	6
Coriander seeds	1½ tsp

Method

Put all these ingredients except the jaggery, in 4 cups of water and bring to a boil. Then let the decoction simmer till it is reduced to one cup. Then add the jaggery, let it dissolve and take off the flame. It can be sipped in small doses through the day.

Makes 2 cups

Holy Basil - Mint Tea

Mint is an excellent carminative and in fact most drugs prescribed for tummy problems contain this ingredient. If you habitually overuse your voice as mothers, teachers or singers do, gargling with his decoction will relieve you of hoarseness. Basil is very effective in preventing all kinds of skin infection and is an antidote for respiratory infections.

Ingredients

Indian basil	10 leaves
Mint	10 leaves
Honey	2 tsp

Method

Put the basil and mint leaves in 4 cups of freshly drawn water and bring to a boil. Let the decoction simmer after it reaches boiling point and is reduced to half the quantity. Take off the flame and mix in honey. Sip this infusion in small doses throughout the day. It is the most soothing expectorant in the world and a refreshing cup of tea too.

Makes 1 cup

Cumin Tea

Herbalists swear by this remedy for getting rid of chronic back pain but personally, the aroma of this tea is what beckons me.

Ingredients	
Cumin, dry roasted and powdered	2 tsp
Ghee	1 tsp
Jaggery to taste	

Method

Put the cumin powder in 4 cups of water and bring to a boil. Then simmer the liquid till it is reduced to one-fourth the quantity. Then add the jaggery, let it dissolve and take off the flame. Add the ghee and drink this up.

Makes 1 cup

Coriander Tea

This tea is one that is most effective when consumed cold rather than hot. It may even help to normalise an excessive bile condition.

Ingredients	
Coriander, dry roasted & powdered	2 tsp
Low fat milk	1 cup
Sugar to taste	

Method

Add the coriander powder to the milk and bring to a boil. Leave to simmer for a couple of minutes. Add sugar to taste and leave to cool to room temperature.

Fenugreek Tea

Serves 1

Fenugreek seeds are rich in iron (16.5 mg/ 100gms) so are a big help in anemia. Apart from which they are also helpful in the treatment of flatulence, colic, dysentery and diarrhoea, sounds almost like the proverbial panacea. But mainly, this tea is recommended for those suffering from hyperacidity. The mucilaginous material deposited by fenugreek passes through the stomach and intestines, providing a protective layer against eroding gastric acids.

Ingredients

Fenugreek seeds	1 tsp
Jaggery to taste	

Method

Put the fenugreek in 2 cups of freshly drawn water and bring to a boil. Let the liquid simmer till it is reduced to half the quantity. Add the jaggery, let it dissolve and take off flame. Strain and sip this tea hot.

SOUPS

Soups are comfort food. When you're feeling under the weather they rejuvenate you entirely, when you feel like spoiling yourself they transform into elegant food, when you want to fill up without really stuffing, they come to your rescue. In hot weather or cold they seduce the senses with their colour and their aroma.

And the beauty of it all is that vegetables which you might otherwise run a mile from, even while knowing that they are good for you, can disguise themselves as the most innocuous ingredient in an otherwise lovely soup. That said, let's get down to the business of making them.

Tomato Soup

Tomatoes, hailed as the modern wonder vegetable for their lycopene content, can be used in a number of ways in a variety of dishes. Luckily for us, lycopene becomes more accessible in the cooked tomato than in the uncooked one. But cooked tomatoes can turn acidic and upset the already sensitive ph balance of our bodies. Hence don't overdo it. Incidentally the fresh celery will counterbalance any acidity caused by the tomatoes.

Ingredients

Tomatoes	½ kg
Ash gourd or bottle gourd	4 inch piece
Carrots	400 gms
Onion	1 medium
Celery, optional	1 stalk
Rock salt to taste	
Pepper powder to taste	
Cumin powder	1 tsp
Oregano to taste	

Method

Wash and roughly chop the vegetables into big pieces. Keep aside a two inch piece of celery for garnish, if you are using it. Skin the gourd and cook with the vegetables.

Cook the whole lot, with 4 cups of water for about 10 minutes. Leave to cool for 10 minutes. Discard the gourd skins and grind the rest in the liquidiser. It is a good idea to have the soup without straining it so as to retain the roughage. But if you are in the mood for a clear soup you may strain it. The carrot pulp has already given it a certain thickness and a wonderful colour so you do not need either cornflour or a colouring agent. If necessary add a tablespoon of soya milk powder, dissolved in water.

Add the desired quantities of salt, pepper, cumin powder and oregano to the soup, mix well and keep covered for 5 minutes so that the oregano infuses with the soup.

Garnish with finely chopped celery or a sprig of coriander and serve hot with garlic bread.

Serves 4-6

Beetroot Soup

Beets are a rich source for the build up of haemoglobin and are helpful in getting rid of constipation. In fact, half of a boiled beetroot consumed every night will keep both these chronic problems at bay. This soup is a very tasty way of consuming the vegetable.

Ingredients

Beetroots	2 medium
Onion	1 small
Plain yogurt	½ cup
Cumin powder	1 tsp
Rock salt to taste	
Pepper powder to taste	
Coriander sprigs for garnish	

Method

Cook the beetroot in its skin, along with the onion and 4 cups of water, till soft. Discard skin and grind in a liquidiser with the onion. Add the yogurt to this and blend well. Add the cumin powder and salt and blend once more. Mix this with the water used for cooking and reheat soup if desired. Sprinkle the pepper powder when you serve in individual bowls. Garnish with coriander sprig and serve. The yogurt substitutes the need for cream very well.

Note:o This soup tastes good when served cold too. Stir it well before serving as the vegetable and the yogurt will separate if kept for too long.

Serves 4-6

Cucumber Soup

The cucumber is 96 per cent water and therefore a natural choice for soups. The alkaline forming minerals in the cucumber represent 64.05 per cent and the acid forming minerals 35.95 per cent. This mineral arrangement makes it useful in maintaining the alkalinity of the blood and a wonderful antidote to acidity. But to put it simply – there is nothing more satisfying than cucumber soup on hot summer days.

Ingredients

Cucumber	½ kg
Plain yogurt	1 cup
Green chillies	4
Cumin powder	1 tsp
Salt to taste	
Green chillies for garnish	

Method

Wash and skin the cucumber. Keep the peels aside for use in chutneys. Chop the cucumber roughly. Deseed two chillies and chop roughly. Grind both in a liquidiser with 2 cups of potable water. Add the yogurt, salt and cumin powder and blend well again. Bring to the correct consistency by adding the water required. Chill for 30 minutes at least. Ladle into soup bowls. Slit the remaining chillies just once lengthwise, deseed them and garnish the soup with these. Be prepared with second helpings, it's so delicious!

Serves 4-6

Spinach Soup

Believe it or not gram for gram, spinach provides the same amount of protein that meat does and it's way cheaper too. It is also the richest source of folic acid, hence invaluable during pregnancy and lactation. But for the body to absorb all its goodness it needs to be helped by generous doses of vitamin C. Therefore, a squeeze of lime is practically statutory.

Ingredients

Spinach	1 bundle
Onion	1 medium
Potato, boiled	1 small
Cumin powder	2 tsp
Rock salt to taste	
Thick yogurt, beaten	1 cup
Pepper powder to taste	
Lime, juiced	1 big

Method

Clean and wash the spinach thoroughly. Cook this along with the onion in 6 cups of water for about 5 minutes. Leave to cool for 10 minutes and then grind in the liquidiser. Blend this with the water used for cooking. Add the cumin powder, lime juice and rock salt and mix well. Do not reheat after mixing the lime juice or the vitamins will be destroyed. Serve in soup bowls garnished with a swirl of beaten yogurt and sprinkle pepper powder.

Clear Soup

Serves 4-6

Recycle vegetable peels, soft centre portions such as those of gourds or pumpkins, hard portions such as those near the root of cauliflower or cabbage or carrot, do not discard them. Store them all in an airtight box in the refrigerator so that they can be used as stock for soups. They can be simmered in six times the quantity of water and strained to obtain clear stock. In case you don't have this in ready stock, just put together a small piece of any gourd or pumpkin and cabbage, a few beans, a small carrot, an onion, a potato and cook them till soft. Leave to cool and grind and strain to obtain stock for soup.

Ingredients

Carrot, diced fine	1 big
French beans, diced fine	10
Finely shredded cabbage	1 cup
Capsicum, chopped into tiny cubes	1 small
Cauliflower, cut into flat florettes	1 cup
Mushrooms, chopped (optional)	5
Tomatoes, chopped	4 medium
Onion, sliced fine	1 medium
Oil of your choice	1 tsp
Soup stock	6 cups
Rock salt and sea salt to taste	
Cumin powder	1 tsp
Curry powder	1 tsp
Pepper powder	1 tsp

Method

Heat the oil in a big thick-bottomed pan and sauté the onions for a minute. Then add the French beans, carrots, cauliflower, mushroom and cabbage and sauté for a couple of minutes more. Then add the soup stock to the vegetables and bring to a boil. Add salt, pepper powder, curry powder, cumin powder and simmer for five minutes only. The vegetables must remain crunchy and retain their original bright colours. Do not cover the pan or the stock will boil over. Just before taking off the flame, add the chopped capsicum. This does not need to cook, it will look good as a garnish but it should get slightly soft just by remaining in the hot soup. Serve immediately. While this soup tastes better on reheating or keeping, it will lose its crunchiness and also the bright colour of its vegetables. It is a great way to get the goodness of all the vegetables without going to the trouble of elaborate cooking. Serve with wholemeal garlic bread.

Serves 4-6

Pumpkin Soup

You could grow viagra in your backyard and never know it. The pumpkin is known to increase virility and is also the richest source of vitamin B among vegetables and fruits. Make sure you buy and use only the mature, ripe variety, never the raw green one. As in other vegetables save the peels and soft centre portion for chutneys and soups.

Ingredients

Pumpkin	½ kg
Onion	1 medium
Tomatoes	2
Garlic	1 clove
Lime, juiced	1
A few sprigs of coriander for garnish	
Red chillie powder	1 tsp
Cumin powder	1 tsp
Pepper powder, optional	1 tsp
Rock salt to taste	
Thick beaten yogurt	½ cup

Method

Wash the pumpkin and skin it. Set the skin aside. Scoop out the soft centre portion along with seeds and keep with the skin. Chop the pumpkin into big pieces. Cook the pumpkin with the onion, tomatoes and garlic along with 3 cups of water. Leave to cool and grind in liquidiser.

Cook the skin and soft centre portion that you've kept aside with 3 cups of water for 10 minutes. Leave to cool and strain this water. Add this stock to the pumpkin paste. Then add the dry powdered spices and mix well.

Serve in soup bowls, pour in a few drops of the limejuice, and add a swirl of the beaten yogurt and garnish with a sprig of coriander.

Serve hot or chilled.

Carrot Soup

After the tomtoming of the beta-carotene content of the carrot, its rich content of calcium must be the world's best kept secret. In fact, if you have this carrot soup one day, carrot juice another day and may be carrot halwa or pudding another day (did you say why not every day?) you would have provided for your body's daily requirement of calcium.

Ingredients

Carrots	400 gms
Onion	1 medium
Coriander for garnish	1 sprig
Rock salt to taste	
Cumin powder	1 tsp
Pepper powder	1 tsp
Soya milk powder	1 tbsp
Or low fat milk	½ cup
Lime, juiced	1
Boiled Corn Nibblets	½ cup

Method

Wash the carrots and scrape off any dirt. Cook the carrots and onion with 5 cups of water till soft. Leave to cool and grind in the liquidiser. Dissolve the soya milk powder in half a cup of water and add to the carrot or add the low fat milk instead. Add the dry spice powder and rock salt and mix well. Serve in soup bowls and then pour a few drops of the lime juice and add a few corn nibblets and a sprig of coriander for garnish. Serve hot or chilled, it tastes great.

Opposite: Carrot Soup

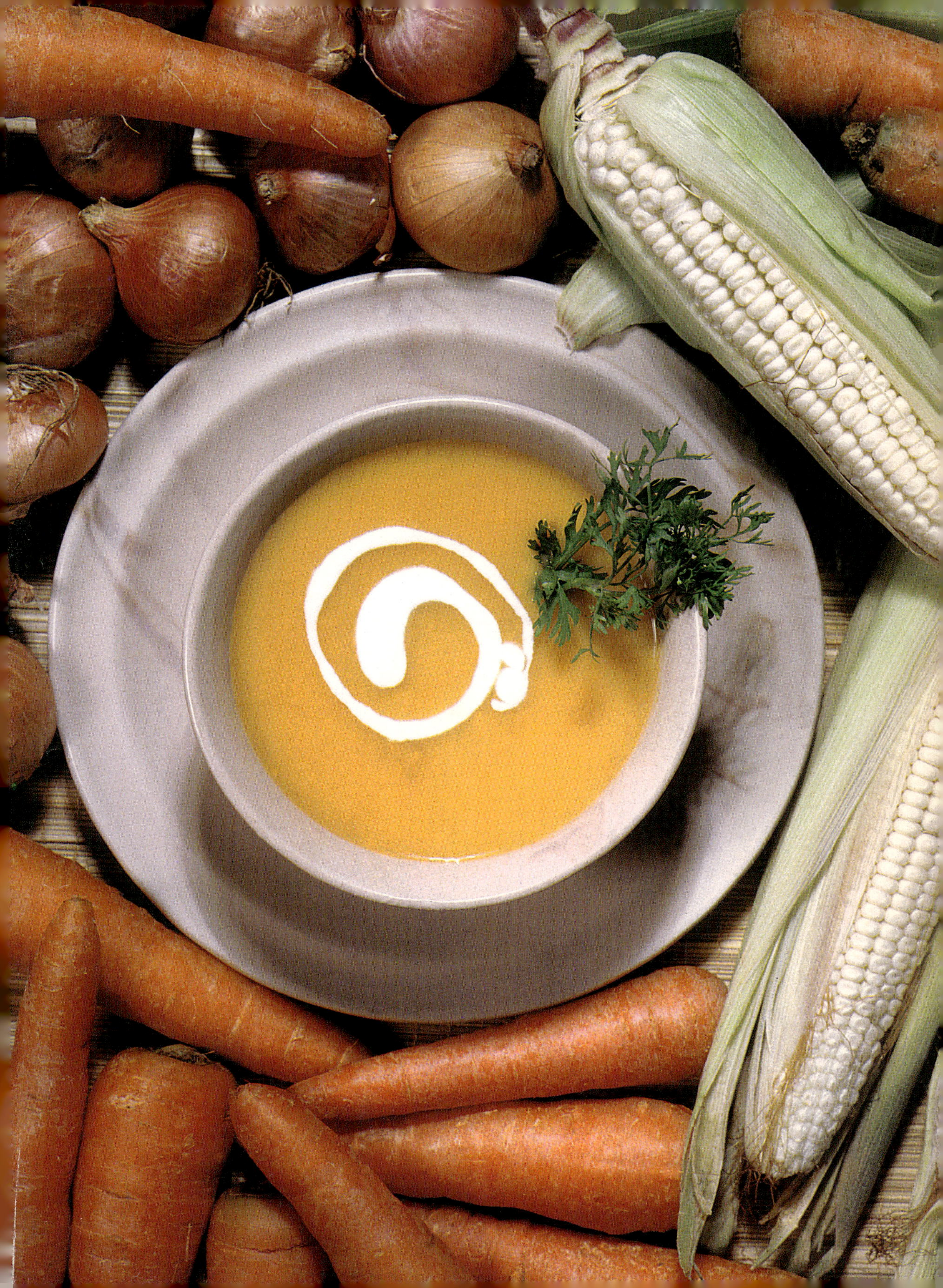

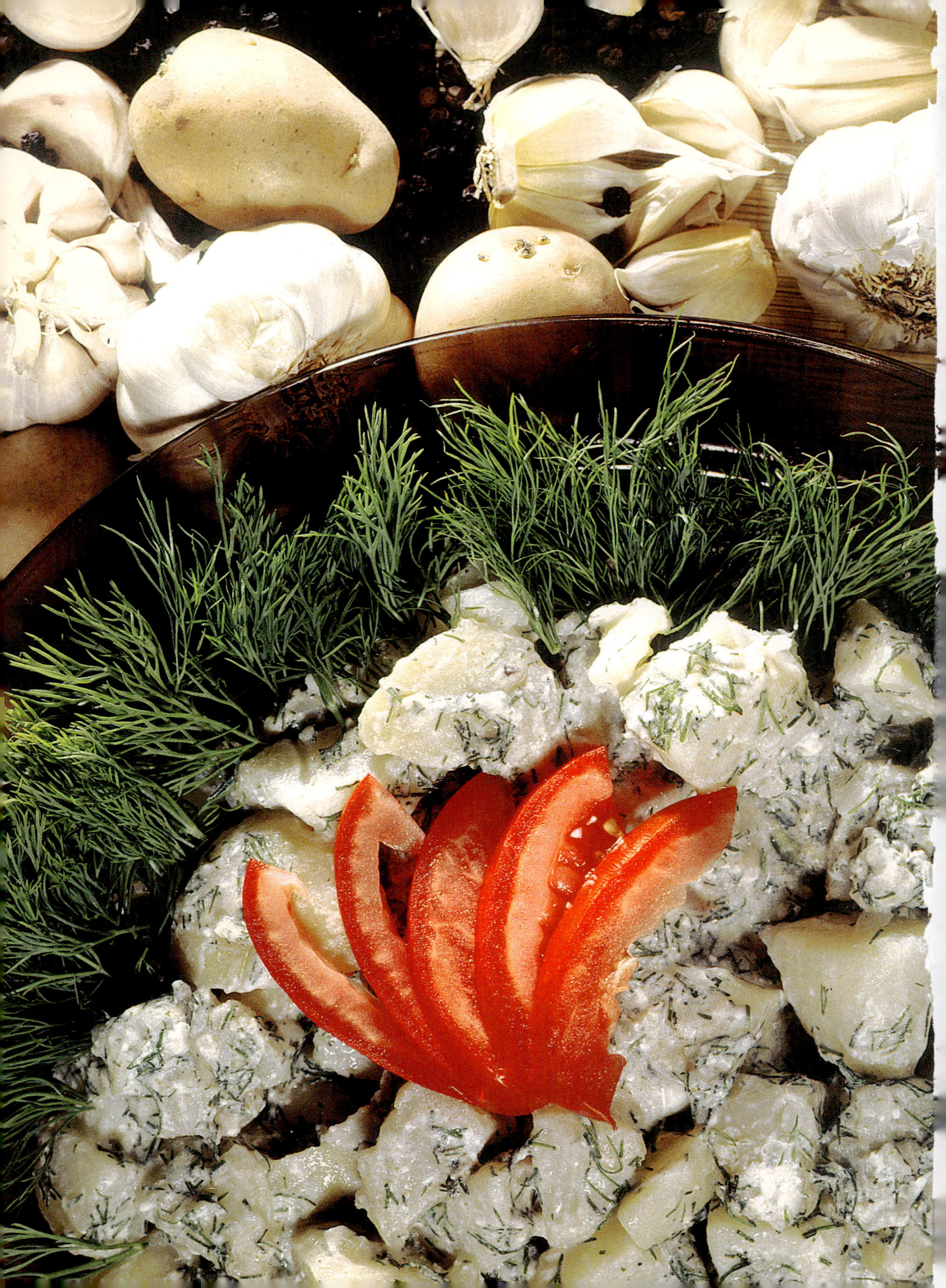

Serves 4-6

Barley – Lentil Soup

While barley is a superior source of protein it is a lot less palatable than corn or beans. The best way to consume it is by adding it to soups, noodles, pasta or even dals. It introduces a natural oily substance, which helps to protect the mucus membrane of the digestive system, making sure that assimilation is improved.

Ingredients

Barley	½ cup
Lentils	¾ cup
Onion, sliced finely	1 medium
Tomatoes, chopped	2
Ginger, chopped	1 inch piece
Rock salt to taste	
Pepper powder to taste	
Fresh coriander, chopped fine for garnish	2 sprigs
A pat of home-made butter (optional)	

Method

Fill a large pan with 6 cups of water and place the barley in it. Bring to a boil and let it simmer for 10–15 minutes.

Clean, wash and add the dal, vegetables and the ginger to the barley and cook till soft. Mash well and adjust salt and pepper to taste. Serve in soup bowls and place a small dab of butter on top if desired. Garnish with the fresh coriander and serve hot.

Opposite: Dill – Potato Salad (ref. page 38)

Snappy-Happy Soup

Serves 4-6

The reason this is included in the soup section is that it combines the best qualities of a soup and a kadhi. Don't let on that it gets done in a jiffy, simply pretend that you feel compelled to make it so often only because it's such a hot favourite with the family. And that will be the truth!

Ingredients

Methkut powder	2 tbsp
Lime, juiced	1
Fresh chopped coriander for garnish	1 tbsp

For the Seasoning

Ghee	½ tsp
Cumin seeds	1 tsp
Curry leaves	5-6
Turmeric powder	½ tsp
Asafoetida	¼ tsp
Green chillie, chopped	1
Black peppercorn	1 tsp
Red chillie powder (optional)	½ tsp
Salt to taste	

Method

Blend the methkut powder in 3 cups of water and set aside. Heat the ghee in a thick-bottomed pan and place the cumin seeds in it. When they start moving around add the rest of the seasoning ingredients and stir fry for a minute. Add 2 cups of water to the pan and bring to a boil. Lower the flame and let it simmer till reduced to half the quantity. Then add the methkut water and bring to a boil once more. Take off the flame and mix in the lime juice. Garnish with the chopped coriander and serve hot with rice or even as an appetiser.

Note: Metkut is a powder made from a mixture of dals. It can be used in a number of ways and can become a staple standby for all occasions. Make this powder a part of your smartly-stocked larder. To make the metkut powder refer to the section on preserves and powders.

Mock Corn Soup
(Bottle Gourd & Barley Soup)

Like most inventions this one too was born out of necessity. A sick child fussing about food. What do I coax him with when I've run out of his favourite sweet corn soup ingredients? Abracadabra a new soup is born. Only it is better, easier to digest and to make.

Ingredients

Barley	1 cup
Bottle gourd, peeled and chopped into big cubes	500 gms
Ripe tomatoes	1 kg
Salt to taste	
Fresh pepper powder	
A few sprigs of parsley or coriander	

Method

The good news is that this soup comes with its own stock. The soft centre portion tastes exactly like the stock used in corn soup because the bottle gourd is in any case one of the main ingredients in the stock. The barley gives the soft chewy feel of the sweet corn. To begin with fill a large pan with 10 cups of water and place the barley in it. Bring it to a boil and let it simmer for 10–15 minutes till the barley is almost cooked.

Then add the bottle gourd and simmer till cooked. Finally add the tomatoes and keep covered for 10 minutes so they become soft in the steam. Then pick out the bottle gourd pieces and the whole tomatoes and grind to a paste in the mixer. Add this paste back to the barley water. Add the seasonings and adjust taste. Garnish with sprigs of parsley or coriander and serve hot.

SALADS IN GRAVIES

Most of us shy away from raw uncooked food because it conjures up vivid pictures of cows chewing cud. While the cows have all day to do it in we, their biped cousins, have to do more than our fair share of rushing about. Now that's exactly why we ought to be eating more raw food – living food, that is. The energy levels we gain from consuming raw food are way above those assimilated from food that has been cooked, grilled, baked or fried. We end up putting away more waste, less nutrition in cooked food. In the case of salads less is more. Less raw food gives you more energy than a similar quantity of cooked food. When you prepare it with the right balance of taste and texture it becomes attractive to the eye and the tongue. Don't pass over this chapter without trying out at least a couple of recipes. That will ensure that you keep coming back for more.

About Salt: If we were to stop and think for a moment about what salt actually comprises of we would probably say sodium chloride. As it happens, the table salt we buy contains a few other chemicals besides this. These are potassium sulphate, sodium sulphate, barium chloride, stontium chloride, magnesium bromide and calcium chloride, in varying proportions. This is because in the commercial production of table salt extremely high temperatures are used, around 750° C, to solidify the salt with additives and adulterants to coat the salt crystals to cause them to pour readily under nearly all conditions. Such salt is not completely water soluble. Since table salt is insoluble in water, it also settles in our bloodstream and hardens our arteries.

The alternative to using table salt is rock salt. Rock salt is found to contain the following elements:

Sodium chloride   90–95%
Calcium sulphate   .05–1%
Magnesium sulphate   .05–1%
Magnesium chloride   .05–1%

The so-called low salt substitute available in the healthfood sections of our supermarket shelves also unfortunately, contain potassium chloride (66% minimum) and magnesium carbonate, the latter used as an anti-caking agent. Perhaps it isn't really an alternative after all.

Rock salt is available at all small and big groceries in the form of natural rock crystals. It can be ground at home to the consistency you desire. It is obtained from soil sodium rock formations and is not subjected to any commercial process. Such rock salt is a natural catalyst which the enzymes in the body can cause to be utilised constructively.

Rock salt has a pungent smell and an attractive flavour when used in raw foods. The ready-to-use masalas like chaat masala, jal jeera masala or kala khatta masala, all contain rock salt. But it is only a matter of time to get used to the taste of rock salt in cooked food. Natural sea salt, available in big crystal form, usually unpackaged, is also a sensible alternative. Perhaps you can use sea salt and rock salt together, in varying proportions till you get used to rock salt exclusively. In any case begin with rock salt in all your salads and you'll automatically switch to using it in cooked food too.

Sprout Gravy with Cabbage

For sheer bulk cabbage wins hands down. It is also abundantly available all over India and almost all over the world. Which also makes it one of the cheaper vegetables. But the reason I like cabbage is the first one. If you are not in the mood for a three course meal, just make yourself this salad – it's light on your stomach and very nourishing at the same time.

Ingredients

Shredded cabbage	2 cups
Finely chopped spring onions with greens	2 cups

For the Gravy

Green mung sprouts	1 cup
Fresh ginger, chopped	1 inch piece
Chopped fresh coriander	1 tbsp
Fresh grated coconut	1 tbsp
Sesame seeds	1 tsp
Cumin seeds	1 tsp
Green chillie	1
Tamarind	1 inch piece
Rock salt to taste	

Method

Grind together all the gravy ingredients to a paste. Transfer the gravy to a glass serving bowl add the shredded cabbage and chopped spring onions. Mix well. Serve immediately.

Coconut Gravy with Brown Sprouted Gram

Gravies take the place of salad dressings in Indian salads. The simplest and least fatty Western dressing is the vinaigrette but the gravies given here are perhaps better for their range of flavours and fortified nutrients.

Ingredients

Sprouted brown gram	2 cups
Shredded cabbage	1 cup
Plain yogurt	1 cup
Cumin powder	1 tsp
Red chillie powder	1 tsp

For the Gravy

Grated fresh coconut	1 cup
Ginger	1 inch piece
Red chillie powder	1 tsp
Curry leaves	4–5
Sesame seeds	1 tsp
Cumin	1 tsp
Rock salt	to taste

Method

Grind all the ingredients for the gravy into a paste. Transfer to a glass serving bowl and beat in the plain yogurt Add the shredded cabbage and sprouted brown gram and mix well. Garnish with cumin and red chillie powder. Serve immediately.

Shredded Carrot in Spinach Gravy

If you are squeamish about eating greens raw for fear of letting e-coli sneak in along with them, you should use the veggie wash available in the market. Alternatively add just 2 drops of chlorine to a bucket of water, let the greens soak for a couple of minutes and rinse out thoroughly. You can wash a whole lot of vegetables in this bucket of water. Though what we need here is just one cup each of spinach and coriander.

Ingredients

Shredded carrot	2 cups
Chopped tomato	1 cup
Grated fresh coconut	1 tbsp

For the Gravy

Chopped spinach	1 cup
Chopped fresh coriander	1 cup
Ginger, chopped	1 inch piece
Green chillie, chopped	1
Lime, juiced	1
Rock salt to taste	

Method

Grind together all the ingredients for the gravy. Transfer to a glass serving dish. Add the shredded carrot and chopped tomato. Mix well. Garnish with the grated coconut and serve immediately.

Serves 4-6

Sprouted Green Gram in Carrot Gravy

This is one good-looking salad. It perks up the table-setting with its bright and contrasting colours. It is especially recommended when you want to make the meal look interesting but don't have the time for decorative garnishes. Just one sprig of coriander in the middle of the pink and green salad will do fine.

Ingredients	
Sprouted green gram	2 cups
Finely chopped onion	1 cup
Chopped fresh coriander	1 tbsp
For the Gravy	
Chopped carrot	2 cups
Grated fresh coconut	1 tbsp
Red chillie powder	1 tsp
Cumin	1 tsp
Lime, juiced	1
Rock salt to taste	

Method

Grind together all the gravy ingredients to a paste. Transfer to a glass serving bowl. Mix in the green gram thoroughly. Garnish with chopped onion and coriander. Serve immediately.

Serves 4-6

Bottle Gourd in Tomato Gravy

If you're lucky you'll have good neighbours. If you're very lucky you'll have the gourd family in your backyard. Each and every member of the gourd family is critical to our good health. You will have noticed almost every home in small towns and sometimes big cities have an ash gourd hanging from the rooftop. Perhaps to ward off the evil eye. But I like to think it is to remind us of the importance of this vegetable in our diet. But in this recipe the bottle gourd plays star. It's different, enjoy it.

Ingredients

Grated bottle gourd	2 cups
Green garlic with leaves, chopped fine	1 cup

For the Gravy

Chopped tomatoes	2 cups
Groundnuts	1 tbsp
Sesame seeds	1 tsp
Cumin	1 tsp
Red chillie powder	1 tsp
Lime, juiced	1
Rock salt to taste	

Method

Choose a tender bottle gourd. Quarter the gourd vertically and grate it. Set aside. Grind all the gravy ingredients to a paste. Transfer to a glass serving bowl. Add the grated bottle gourd, chopped green garlic and mix well. Serve immediately.

Serves 4-6

Sprouted Mung in Tomato Gravy

The mung bean is a versatile seed. If I had to choose one must-have item in my refrigerator it would be the sprouted mung bean. It makes an excellent starter as a salad, a gravy if you are in the mood for it, can move into a paratha if called upon, will unobtrusively mingle in a khichdi, or serve as a great garnish on any savoury snack. Give it life membership in your chill tray and you'll be amazed at the variety of ways in which you can serve it. There's a corollary, however, don't let it sit for more than 3 – 4 days.

Ingredients

Sprouted mung	2 cups
Plain yogurt	1 cup
Fresh coriander, chopped fine	1 tbsp

For the Gravy

Chopped tomatoes	2 cups
Groundnuts	1 tbsp
Fresh ginger	1 inch piece
Curry leaves	4–5
Sesame seeds	1 tsp
Cumin	1 tsp
Red chillie powder	1 tsp
Rock salt to taste	

Method

Grind all the gravy ingredients to a paste. Transfer to a glass serving bowl. Beat the yogurt and add to the gravy. Then mix in the sprouted mung. Garnish with fresh coriander and serve immediately.

Cauliflower in Onion Gravy

A little-known secret of the cauliflower is the substantial content of vitamin C that it has. Eating it raw in a salad will allow us to get the full benefit of this. The onion gravy gives this otherwise bland vegetable a sharp edge.

Ingredients

Grated cauliflower	2 cups
Green chillie, deseeded, chopped fine	1
Chopped fresh coriander	1 tbsp

For the Gravy

Chopped onion	1 cup
Chopped tomato	2 cups
Garlic	1 clove
Cumin	1 tsp
Black pepper powder	¼ tsp
Cinnamon	1 inch piece
Cloves	2
Rock salt to taste	

Method

Grind together all the gravy ingredients to a paste. Transfer to a glass serving bowl. Add to this the grated cauliflower and chopped green chillie. Mix well. Garnish with fresh coriander and serve immediately.

Serves 4-6

Cucumber in Green Gravy

All the ingredients of the bhel-puri minus the sinful ones. And the lovely green of this cucumber-mint salad will make it the ideal summer starter. Make sure there's enough to go around, you'll want second helpings.

Ingredients	
Diced cucumber	2 cups
Raw mango, chopped fine	1 cup
For the Gravy	
Chopped fresh coriander	1 cup
Chopped mint	1 cup
Fresh ginger	1 inch piece
Cumin	1 tsp
Green chillie, chopped	1
Rock salt to taste	

Method

Grind all the gravy ingredients to a paste. Transfer to a glass serving bowl. Mix in the diced cucumber and chopped raw mango. Serve immediately.

Bottle Gourd in Green Garlic Gravy

The garlic pod is endowed with miraculous health properties and as always the raw state is the best. Teamed with the bottle gourd it provides the right foil to the mild-mannered vegetable.

Ingredients

Grated bottle gourd	2 cups
Grated fresh coconut	1 cup

For the Gravy

Chopped green garlic with stalk	1 cup
Chopped tomato	1 cup
Chopped carrot	1 cup
Ginger, chopped	1 inch piece
Cumin	1 tsp
Green chillie, chopped	1

Method

Grind all the gravy ingredients to a paste. Transfer to a glass serving bowl. Choose a tender bottle gourd and peel skin only if necessary and grate the gourd. Mix this into the gravy. Garnish with fresh coconut and serve immediately.

Serves 4-6

Cabbage in Capsicum Gravy

The capsicum or the bell pepper comes in green, red and yellow colours though in India we are mostly familiar with the green. It also has the highest content of vitamin C among vegetables. In the gravy it loses its crunchy texture so if you wish you can keep a few juliennes of capsicum to add to the salad.

Ingredients

Finely chopped cabbage	2 cups
Groundnuts, soaked in water for 30 minutes	1 cup
Chopped cashew nuts	1 tbsp

For the Gravy

Capsicum, deseeded and chopped	1 big
Grated fresh coconut	1 tbsp
Chopped fresh coriander	1 tbsp
Sesame seeds	1 tsp
Red chillie powder	1 tsp
Lime, juiced	1
Black pepper powder	¼ tsp
Rock salt to taste	

Method

Grind all the gravy ingredients to a paste. Transfer to a glass serving bowl. Mix in the chopped cabbage and soaked groundnuts. Garnish with chopped cashew nuts and serve immediately.

SALAD BAR - CRUNCHES AND CURLS

Believe me, it's possible to get high on this. The clean and light feeling that you get when you make salads a part of every major meal in itself becomes habit forming. Then you will not need the gurus of good health to remind you of your daily requirement of living food. This has been my experience as also of those others who have tried it out for even a few days. So you only have to try it and the rest is accomplished on its own. I'll let you in on a personal anecdote. When I joined a weekend newspaper as their health and cuisine editor, they expected me to sort of live out a gourmet gastronomic life. But did I disappoint them! For there was I at every lunch hour gorging on my salad box before I got to the main meal. It wasn't long before my colleagues started attacking my salad box. Soon I had to fight for own share of the salad. But, and this is the most gratifying part – before I left the job to move to another city, my colleagues had become converts to carrying home-cooked lunch. And what do you think it comprised? Salads!

The cost benefit ratio in salads is mind-boggling – they cost you little in terms of calories but the energy levels you derive from them are tremendous. What's more, all you need in terms of an investment is a food processor with a chopper attachment and 10 minutes of your time. Let's go!

Dill Potato Salad

Serves 4-6

Potato is not in the top 10 of most nutritionists' fave lists. In fact, Michael Montignac has made it his mission in life to educate us about the drastic unhealthy effects of the spud. His reasoning is that it has a high glycaemic index and in people prone to overweight it helps in escalating the problem. However, a little bit of the spud eaten the right way can do no harm. On the contrary it will help you keep to the middle path after a little gratification.

Ingredients

Potatoes, boiled	4 medium
Dill, chopped fine	1 tbsp
Plain yogurt, beaten	1 cup
Cumin powder	1 tsp heaped
Pepper powder	½ tsp
Rock salt to taste	

Method

Peel and dice the boiled potatoes. Add the chopped dill and the rest of the ingredients as well. Mix well, check and adjust the seasoning. Let it sit for about 15 minutes and serve with sandwiches.

Mung and Carrot Salad

This is my neice Anushree's favourite salad. She came across the salad when she was beginning to take an interest in cooking and this turned out to be a launching pad. Ever since this is part of her favourite menu.

Ingredients

Mung sprouts	1 cup
Shredded carrot	1 cup
Onion, chopped fine	1 medium
Lime, juiced	1
Cumin powder	1 tsp
Pepper powder	1 tsp
Rock salt to taste	
Finely chopped coriander, for garnish	1 tbsp

Method

The thing to do is just put all the ingredients in a glass serving bowl. Toss the whole lot together. Garnish with the coriander and serve immediately.

Cabbage Walnut Salad

Serves 4-6

This salad is a favourite with kids and those with a sweet tooth. It's delicious. Don't worry about the calories from walnuts and cottage cheese – think about the cabbage, it has an enzyme that cleans out the cholesterol.

Ingredients

Shredded cabbage	2 cups
Chopped walnut	1 cup
Diced cottage cheese	1 cup
Raisins	1 tbsp
Lime, juiced	1
Rock salt to taste	

Method

Make sure you choose a crisp and fresh cabbage. Put in all the ingredients, except the walnuts, into a glass serving bowl and toss them well. Garnish with the walnuts and chill for 30 minutes. Serve as a side dish with any food – Indian, Continental or Chinese – it compliments every kind of cuisine.

Green Gram & Green Mango Salad

This tangy, tantalising chaat sold on the beaches from Mumbai to Chennai simply seduces your tastebuds. Each city will have it's own variation – in Chennai it is garnished with succulent coconut gratings. Make this a must on your short eats menu – a favourite with all ages.

Ingredients

Sprouted green gram	2 cups
Green mango, chopped fine with skin	1 medium
Onion, chopped fine	1 medium
Finely chopped fresh coriander	1 tbsp
Curry leaves	4–5
Turmeric powder	½ tsp
Asafoetida	¼ tsp
Green chillie, deseeded and finely chopped	1
Rock salt to taste	

Method

Cook the green gram with the curry leaves, asafoetida, turmeric powder, sea salt and rock salt in the desired proportion, for 10–15 minutes till tender. Leave to cool.

Transfer the cooked gram to a glass serving bowl and add the mango, onion and green chillie. Check and adjust seasoning. Garnish with fresh coriander and serve at room temperature.

Brown Gram and Coconut Salad

Serves 4-6

The sprouted brown gram has a slight edge over the green gram – it has plenty of vitamin B complex and iron.

Ingredients

Sprouted brown gram	2 cups
Grated coconut	½ cup
Green chillie, deseeded and chopped fine	1
Curry leaves	4–5
Tamarind	2 inch piece
Turmeric powder	½ tsp
Asafoetida	¼ tsp
Sea salt and Rock salt to taste	

Method

Add the curry leaves, turmeric powder, asafoetida, tamarind and the salts in the desired proportion and adequate water to the sprouted brown gram and cook for 10–15 minutes or till tender. When cool pick out the tamarind and dispose.

Transfer the mixture to a glass serving bowl, minus the water, and add the green chillie and half the quantity of coconut. Mix well. Garnish with the remaining coconut and serve at room temperature.

Serves 4-6

Pure White Ecstasy

The ash gourd was the most wanted vegetable among the ancient ascetics of India. It is called brain food. Due to its water content it is also the most easily digestible source of minerals and vitamins. It is best to make this a part of your daily diet. What's more it is also very versatile in that no part of it is wasted. The peel is used in tantalising chutney form and the soft centre portion makes excellent soup stock. Here it is used raw, the ideal way to conserve and use its excellent nutritive properties.

Ingredients

Ash gourd	500 gms
Fresh coconut, grated	2 tbsp
Bean sprouts	1 cup
Cumin powder	2 tsp
Ginger, grated	1 inch
Lime, juiced	1
Finely chopped fresh coriander	1 tbsp
Peanuts, soaked overnight	1 tbsp
Rock salt to taste	

Method

Skin the ash gourd and store the peels for use later in a chutney. Chop off the soft centre portion with seeds and store this separately for use in a soup stock.

Cut the gourd into quarters and chop finely as you would a big sized onion. If you find chopping difficult, grate it or mince in a food processor. These processes will, however, make the pulp watery therefore chopping is recommended.

Transfer the chopped ash gourd to a glass serving bowl and add all the other ingredients, except the fresh coriander. Mix well. Garnish with fresh coriander and serve immediately.

Date with Cabbages

Cabbage has an enzyme which is highly effective in giving a healthy glow to your hair and skin. Dates are a rich source of calcium and aid in the proper development of bones, teeth and muscle activity, for example that of the heart.

Ingredients

Shredded cabbage	2 cups
Sprouted mung	1 cup
Dates, deseeded and sliced fine	2 tbsp
Lime, juiced	1
Pepper powder	1 tsp
Cumin powder	1 tsp
Rock salt to taste	

Method

Make sure you pick a fresh and crisp cabbage. Mix the shredded cabbage with half the quantity of dates and the rest of the ingredients in a serving bowl. Toss well. Check and adjust seasoning. Garnish with the rest of the dates and serve immediately.

This makes great fasting food.

Serves 4-6

Serves 4-6

Crunches Crunch (Banana Stem Salad)

This is the crunchiest salad I have come across, even better than cabbage, mainly because it is moisture laden. Make sure that the stem is fresh – light brown at the ends and milky white all over. Press the stem to feel the freshness. This is a rich source of calcium and iron – invaluable for females of all ages. Also it contains rich amounts of soluble fibre and leaves one feeling light the morning after. It is an ideal antidote to bingeing on junk food.

Ingredients

Fresh banana stem, chopped fine	6 inches long
Ginger, chopped fine	1 inch piece
Green chillie, deseeded and chopped fine	1
Finely chopped fresh corainder	1 tbsp
Fresh, grated coconut	1 tbsp
Lime, juiced	1
Rock salt to taste	
Buttermilk Or lime juiced	1 tbsp

For the Seasoning

Oil of your choice	2 tsp
Mustard seeds	1 tsp
Fenugreek seeds	¼ tsp
Asafoetida	¼ tsp
Split black gram	1 tsp
Curry leaves	4–5

Method

This salad requires a little bit of technique. Before you begin take a bowl of clean water to which you add either the lime juice or buttermilk. Chop the stem into this bowl of water to preventing it from discolouring. You may have to peel off the outer layers if they are dried and brittle. Then cut the stem into ¼ inch thick roundels and wind the loose fibre round your finger to dispose off later. Put these roundels into the bowl of water immediately. Remove 4–5 roundels at a time and pile them on top of each other and chop fine. Transfer the chopped stem to a glass serving bowl and mix in the lime juice immediately. Then prepare the seasoning. Heat the oil in a small seasoning pan and add the mustard. When it splutters add the rest of the seasoning ingredients. Stir fry for a minute and take off heat. Pour the seasoning over the chopped stem. Add the chopped chillie, ginger, coconut and rock salt and toss thoroughly to mix well. Garnish with chopped coriander and serve at room temperature. It goes well with any variety of rice and tastes good as a mid-morning snack too.

Not So Crunchy

This is an alternative method of preparing the banana stem salad for those who prefer less crunchy food.

Ingredients

Banana stem	6 inches long
Buttermilk	1 cup
Cumin powder	1 tsp
Fresh chopped coriander	1 tbsp
Rock salt to taste	

Method

Chop the banana stem using the same method as the earlier recipe. Then in a thick-bottomed pan put in the buttermilk and the banana stem and cook covered for about 5 minutes. Then stir in the rock salt and cumin powder and close the pan. Take off the flame. After 5 minutes garnish with chopped coriander and serve hot.

Note: This recipe is particularly suited when the banana stem is not too tender.

Serves 4-6

Fenugreek Salad

Fenugreek seeds when sprouted lose most of the bitterness that they contain. They are a rich source of iron and calcium and this salad is recommended for nursing mothers whose reserves of these nutrients are chronically low.

Ingredients

Sprouted fenugreek seeds	1 cup
Grated fresh coconut	1 cup
Jaggery, sliced fine	½ cup
Rock salt to taste	

Method

The method of sprouting fenugreek seeds is the same as for other seeds. Clean, wash and soak the seeds in adequate water for 24 hours. Change the water as often as you can, at least 3–4 times. This leaves the seeds smelling fresh. Then drain and leave to germinate for 12 hours. The exact amount of time taken to germinate will largely depend on the weather in your part of the world.

Preparing this salad is fairly simple. Put all the ingredients together in a serving bowl. Set aside for 15 minutes so that the jaggery blends with the other ingredients. Serve with hot rice or rotis. It can even be had alongside any snack. Obviously you can't eat a whole lot of this salad. But it is very helpful to make this a regular part of your diet. Once a week is a great idea for all of us.

Note: The best way to integrate fenugreek sprouts into your daily diet is to soak them along with any other seeds. Add about 1 tablespoon of fenugreek seeds to 1 cup of other seeds.

Cucumber Mung Salad

Serves 4-6

This is a salad you can prepare when you've run out of sprouts and can't do without living food on your menu. It is prepared with split yellow mung. There is nothing to beat this combination for fresh tangy taste. Try it once and you'll get hooked on it, like my son Sanjit. He literally makes a meal out of it!

Ingredients

Split yellow mung	1 cup
Minced cucumber	2 cups
Fresh grated coconut	1 tbsp
Finely chopped fresh coriander	1 tbsp
Chillie, deseeded and chopped fine	1
Rock salt to taste	
Lime, juiced Or	1
Raw mango, chopped fine	1

For the Seasoning

Oil of your choice	1 tsp
Mustard seeds	1 tsp
Turmeric powder	¼ tsp
A pinch of asafoetida	
Curry leaves	4–5
Fenugreek seeds	¼ tsp

Method

Clean, wash and soak the mung dal in 2 cups of potable water for an hour. The mung will absorb the water and puff up. Drain any excess water.

Transfer the mung to a serving bowl. Add the cucumber, half the quantity of the coconut, ginger, green chillie and rock salt. Mix well.

To prepare the seasoning, heat the oil in a seasoning pan and add the mustard seeds to it. When they splutter, add the rest of the seasoning ingredients, stir for a minute and take off the flame.

Pour the seasoning onto the mixture. Add the lime juice and toss well to mix.

Garnish with remaining coconut and serve immediately.

Serves 4-6

Lettuce Tomato Salad

This is ideal for hot summer days when you need all the liquid nourishment you can get.

Ingredients

Chopped lettuce	2 cups
Tomatoes, cubed	4 medium
Shredded cabbage	2 cups
Dried mango powder	1 tsp
Cumin powder	1 tsp
Rock salt to taste	

Method

Put in all the ingredients in a glass serving bowl and toss well to mix thoroughly. Chill for 15 minutes so that the juices get to know each other well. Serve alongside sandwiches or make a meal of this.

Colourful Entrée

A salad with the most easily available ingredients that appeases every palate.

Ingredients

Diced cucumber	1 cup
Cubed tomato	1 cup
Grated carrot	1 cup
Finely chopped onion	1 cup
Chopped fresh coriander	1 tbsp
Cumin powder	1 tsp
Lime, juiced	1
Pepper powder	1 tsp
Rock salt to taste	

Method

Put together all the ingredients, except the coriander, in a glass serving bowl and toss well to mix. Garnish with the coriander and serve immediately.

Serves 4-6

Mung Peanut Tomato Salad

A high protein salad that is also easily digestible because it comes from germinated sources and has a delicious nutty texture and flavour.

Ingredients

Sprouted mung	1 cup
Sprouted peanuts	1 tbsp
Cubed tomato	1 cup
Fresh grated coconut (optional)	1 tbsp
Finely chopped fresh coriander	1 tbsp
Cumin powder	1 tsp
Green chillie, deseeded and chopped fine	1
Lime, juiced	1
Rock salt to taste	

Method

It is as easy to sprout peanuts as it is to sprout green mung or red. Add the peanuts to the mung when you clean, wash and soak them. Change the water in the soaking stage at least three times, more often if the weather is hot. Drain and leave to germinate. The peanuts will take about 24 hours to show shoots but if you wish to consume them earlier, as the mung will sprout in just eight hours after draining the water, you can eat them.

Assemble all the ingredients, except the coconut and coriander, together in a glass serving bowl and toss well to mix. Garnish with coconut and coriander and serve immediately.

Knol Khol Tomato Salad

Certain vegetables like cabbage, turnips and radish give out a certain smell when cooked, whereas in their raw state they have a fresh and pungent odour. For this very reason salads prepared with these vegetables come as a pleasant surprise.

Ingredients

Knol khol, skinned and diced	1
Tomatoes, cubed	4
Green mango, cubed	1
Sprouted mung	1 cup
Cucumber, diced	1
Finely chopped fresh coriander	1 tbsp
Lime, juiced	1
Red chillie powder	½ tsp
Rock salt to taste	

Method

Make sure you choose a tender crisp knol khol. Skin it and cut into quarters. Then dice it.

Assemble all the ingredients, except the coriander, in a glass serving bowl. Toss well to mix. Garnish with coriander and serve immediately.

Serves 4-6

Signal Salad

Stop says the RED; Go says the GREEN; Get ready says the ORANGE, standing in between!

This nursery rhyme is a good description for this salad because you are using capsicum of all three colours. While earlier red and and yellow bell peppers were not to be seen in the Indian markets, except for hilly areas, with the global kitchen invasion they have now reached all city markets.

Ingredients

Green bell pepper, cubed	1 big
Red bell pepper, cubed	1 big
Yellow bell pepper, cubed	1 big
Finely chopped scallion (spring onion) stalks	1 cup
Scallions, chopped in rings	1 cup
Cubed tomatoes	2 cups
Celery, chopped in 1 inch pieces (optional)	1 stalk
Extra virgin olive oil Or oil of your choice	1 tbsp
Balsamic vinegarx	1 tbsp
Or Lime, juiced	1
Pepper, freshly ground	½ tsp
Rock salt to taste	

Method

Assemble all the ingredients, except the scallion stalks, in a glass serving bowl and toss to mix well. Garnish with the scallion stalks. Cover with cling film and chill for 30 minutes. Serve alongside pasta or sandwiches.

Ready ways with Radish

Serves 4-6

The sharp pungent taste of radish is tamed just right by the nutty flavours of the cumin and the onion seeds. Choose a radish that is translucent white right to its core, discard those that are opaque white, particularly at the core.

Ingredients

Radish, washed and scraped	1
For the Gravy	
Chopped fresh coriander	1 cup
Lime, juiced	1
Jeera	1 tsp
Onion seeds	1 tsp
Rock salt to taste	

Method

Make a paste of the gravy ingredients. Chop the radish into juliennes. Mix into the chopped radish and let it sit for 15 minutes. Serve with main meals or even as cocktail starters.

Radish with a Western Accent

Radish leaves have more calcium, phosphorus, vitamin C and protein than the radish itself. So try and use the leaves in the salad as well.

Ingredients

Radish, washed and scraped	1
A few tender radish leaves, washed and chopped fine	
Plain yogurt	1 cup
Chopped parsely	1 cup
Ringed spring onions	1 cup
Lime, juiced	½
Green chillie chopped	1
Rock salt to taste	

Method

Whisk the yogurt till it turns uniformly smooth. Add the onions, chillie, parsely, rock salt and mix well. Then add the lime juice and mix again.

Finally add the radish and mix till it is well coated with the yoghurt. Chill for 30 minutes. Serve alongside Western style cuisine or even Indian style.

Cucumber with Tofu

Serves 4-6

Compared to the eat-them-on-the-go salads, this one is a gourmet item. You need a little extra time on hand to prepare and savour this salad. Once you taste it you'll make sure you have it often.

Ingredients

Ingredient	Quantity
Cucumber	1
Crumbled tofu	1 cup
Olive oil	2 tsp
Red chillie powder	1 tsp
Lime juice	2 tbsp
Chopped fresh coriander	1 cup
Chillie, chopped	1 green
Papads, roasted	2
Grated Parmesan cheese	1 tbsp
Rock salt to taste	

Method

Heat the olive oil in a saucepan and add the tofu to it. Stir fry for a minute and then add the rock salt, red chillie powder and stir fry till the fat oozes out of the tofu. Leave to cool. Chop the cucumber in the middle lengthwise and then cut into roundels. In a big bowl put in the cooled tofu and the cucumber and add the coriander, rock salt, lime juice and green chillies and mix well. Break the roasted papad into medium sized pieces and mix it with the tofu cucumber salad just before serving. Garnish with the grated cheese. Makes a great evening snack or a meal by itself if you are in the mood for a light, nourishing meal which tingles the taste buds.

Note: You can substitute the tofu with cottage cheese if you wish, though tofu has zero cholesterol and more calcium.

Serves 4-6

Cauliflower Salad

Cauliflower is a rich source of vitamin B6- pyridoxine and choline. Pyridoxine has been found beneficial in the treatment of morning sickness and travel sickness. Of course, you will know the right dose only on medical advice but this salad could add to your resources. It also has a crunchy texture and tangy taste.

Ingredients

Grated cauliflower	2 cups
Plump green chillie, deseeded, chopped fine	1
Finely chopped coriander	1 tbsp
Lime, juiced	1
Rock salt to taste	

Method

Soak the cauliflower in hot salted water for 10 minutes and clean thoroughly before grating. Mix the lime juice, chillie and rock salt into the grated cauliflower. Transfer to a glass serving bowl. Garnish with fresh coriander and serve immediately.

Tomatoes with Roasted Split Chick Peas

This is another traditional salad which evokes in me the memory of huge gatherings, a communal preparation of food and laughter and fun through the day.

Ingredients

Tomatoes, cubed	4 medium
Roasted split chick peas	1 cup
Green chillie, chopped	1
Fresh chopped coriander	1 tbsp
Rock salt to taste	

Method

This one gets done practically before you can say tomato salad. Roasted split chick peas are also known as *puthana* in Marathi, *puttu kadalai* in Tamil or *dalia* in Hindi.

Dry grind the roasted split chick peas along with the green chillie coarsely. Mix this with the cubed tomatoes and the rock salt. Transfer to a serving bowl and garnish with the chopped coriander. Serve with either rice or rotis.

VEGGIE BAZAR – HOW GREEN IS MY VALLEY ...AND RED AND PURPLE

Suddenly it is fashionable to be a vegan. For years the beleaguered Indian tourist used to wear out his footwear and his wallet in search of some vegetarian fare abroad. With the increasing awareness of the benefits of vegetarianism, helped greatly by celebrities like Paul Macartney launching their signature vegan products, you are more likely to find veggie meals on restaurant menus, at least in the US.

What do we find happening in our country? Our *dhabas* around the corner that originally supplied piping hot samosas and tantalising *chaat* are increasingly being taken over by the fast food chains. While global exposure is a good thing to happen to a developing country like ours, we conveniently ignore the more relevant global happenings.

Why, for example have we never read about Dr C Koop, former US surgeon general, and his path breaking report on vegetarianism as the only alternative to good health? His report was based on 2,000 scientific studies of the most rigorous nature and was published more than a decade ago in 1988. It says that if you remove suicide and unintentional injuries such as vehicle accidents from the list of causes, the number of deaths to which diet is a contributing factor is a whopping 80 per cent. The chief factors are pointed out to be saturated fats and cholesterol eaten in disproportionate amounts. The source of these are the animal products – meat, poultry, fish, eggs and even dairy foods. The surgeon general recommends that you reduce your intake of animal products while increasing your intake of fruit, vegetables and whole grains.

And if this recommendation were not enough we have a list of highly creative and successful people who lived a vegan lifestyle beginning with Leonardo da Vinci, Benjamin Franklin, Albert Einstein, George Bernard Shaw, Socrates and our very own Amitabh Bachchan.

Ash Gourd Quickie

Serves 4-6

Ash gourd is said to enhance the mental powers. It is equally true that it is tremendously easy on the digestion and therefore frees our energy to go on to other important processes. The taste of the herbs added is just a shade strong, enough to offset the mild flavour of this vegetable. It is very good convalescent food but I also make this when I am looking for a light meal to rest the digestion after a bout of indulgence.

Ingredients

Ash gourd, skinned, cubed	500 gms
Ginger	1 inch piece
Curry leaves	6
Chillie, chopped	1
Grated fresh coconut	2 tbsp
Tomato, cubed	1 medium
Mustard seeds	1 tsp
Asafoetida	¼ tsp
Turmeric powder	½ tsp
Fenugreek seeds	5–6
Chopped fresh coriander	1 tbsp
Oil of our choice	1 tsp
Salt to taste	

Method

When you skin the ash gourd set aside the skin to make chutney. Discard the seeds in the soft centre portion. You may use the soft portion if you like but since it turns into a mash when cooked, you can keep it aside for use in soup stock later. Cube the firm portion of the gourd. Though it seems like a large part of the gourd is not used in this curry you can actually put it all to use in other tasty and nourishing ways.

Heat the oil in a heavy bottomed pan and make a seasoning of mustard, asafoetida, fenugreek seeds, curry leaves and turmeric powder. Setting aside the coriander, add the rest of the ingredients and mix well. Add half a cup of water only, since the vegetable will release enough moisture. Steam the vegetable either in a rice cooker or prepare it in the usual way in a kadhai.

Steaming gives better results both in terms of the look and taste. Leave to cool and transfer to a serving bowl. Garnish with chopped coriander and serve hot with rotis or rice.

Serves 4-6

Red Spinach with Peanuts

This is known as maath in India but red spinach elsewhere. Unlike spinach it has no distinguishing taste but combined with crushed peanuts it has a very attractive flavour. As in all deep coloured vegetables, the nutrirtional benefits of vitamin A and iron are high.

Ingredients

Red spinach	1 bundle
Raw unsalted peanuts, crushed	1 cup
Grated fresh coconut	2 tsp
Tamarind	1 lemon sized ball
Red chille powder	1 tsp
Or to taste	
Salt to taste	
Oil of your choice	1 tsp
Mustard seeds	1 tsp
Asafoetida	¼ tsp
Turmeric powder	½ tsp

Method

Soak the tamarind in a cup of water for 10 minutes and extract the juice. Set aside.

Clean thoroughly and wash the leaves in running water. Chop the leaves as you would for spinach. Place the mustard and oil in a pan and when the mustard splutters add the asafoetida and the turmeric powder. Then add the chopped leaves and the rest of the ingredients, setting aside 2 tsp of coconut for garnish. Add 1 cup of water only since the vegetable will release moisture, and mix well. Cook for 5 minutes or till cooked. Allow it to cool. Transfer to a serving bowl and garnish with the grated coconut. Serve hot with rotis or rice. You might want to add more water if you are serving this with rice. Or perhaps you might even want to eat this by itself. It's delicious.

Bright Vegetables in Coconut Gravy

This stew looks a riot of colour. Orange carrots, green beans, fresh peas, translucent onions, black pepper, a few deceptive pieces of green chillies all giving you the come hither against a creamy white background.

Ingredients

Chopped carrots	1 cup
Chopped French beans	1 cup
Fresh or frozen peas	1 cup
Fresh or frozen corn, optional	1 cup
Onion, sliced	1 medium
Coconut milk powder	5 tbsp
Or Coconut cream	3½ cups
Green chillies, deseeded and chopped	2
Black peppercorns	1 tsp
Cumin seeds	1 tsp
Curry leaves	5–6
Oil of your choice	1 tsp
Salt to taste	

Method

Dilute the coconut milk powder in an equal quantity of water. Heat the oil in a flat-bottomed pan. Place the cumin in it, when it starts moving around add the chillies, curry leaves and peppercorn. Stir fry for a minute.

Add all the vegetables, and immediately add half the quantity of coconut milk. Cover the pan and cook for 5 minutes or till the vegetables are partially cooked. Then add the salt and the balance coconut milk and cook for a couple of minutes more. While the vegetables should be cooked, they should also retain their bright colour and remain crisp.

Transfer to a glass serving bowl so as to show off this multi-coloured vegetable stew. The mix is so colourful that it does not need a garnish. Serve hot with rotis or rice.

Serves 4-6

Dill Se

Yam has an exceptionally high-fibre content. While this makes it a must on our weekly menu, it also makes us prime candidates for flatulence. Dill is an effective carminative. Together they make a winning combination.

Ingredients

Dill	1 bunch
Yam, skinned and cubed	400 gms
Onion, chopped fine	1 medium
Garlic, peeled and minced	4 cloves
Ginger, chopped	1 inch piece
Tamarind	1 lemon sized ball
Cumin seeds	2 tsp
Bishops weed	1 tsp
Turmeric powder	1 tsp
Chillie powder	1 tsp
Asafoetida	1 tsp
Oil of your choice	2 tsp
Onion, sliced thinly	1 small

Method

Soak the tamarind in a cup of water for at least 10 minutes to extract juice.

Wash thoroughly and clean the yam before skinning and cubing it. Rub a little tamarind water on our hands to prevent any itch the yam may cause.

Heat the oil in a pan and place the cumin seeds in it. When they begin to move add the turmeric powder, asafoetida and bishop's weed. Stir fry for 10 seconds and add the minced garlic and chopped onion. Stir-fry till the onion turns translucent and put in the tamarind extract. Add a cup of plain water and then the yam and dill. Lastly add the salt. Mix well and cook the vegetables till they are soft. Leave to cool. Mash well so that the tastes and flavours are well-blended. Transfer to a serving dish and garnish with the sliced onion. Serve hot with plain phulkas and a raita.

Serves 4-6

Baby Boom

This veggie dish is a treat to see and it also gets done in a jiffy. Do not underestimate the power of visual suggesstion. I have experienced a sudden spurt of growling stomachs where before there were "not hungry" protestations. That's how this dish works.

Ingredients

Baby brinjals, halved	8
Baby tomatoes, halved	4
Baby onions	6
Coriander powder	2 tbsp
Cumin powder	½ tbsp
Red chillie powder	1 tsp
Peanuts, roasted and crushed	2 tbsp
Finely chopped fresh coriander	1 tbsp
Salt to taste	
Oil of your choice	2 tsp

Method

Heat the oil in a pan and sauté the onions. Then add the halved brinjals and tomatoes and dry spices and cook covered till the brinjals are cooked but not mushy or soft. Add a little water if required. It is better to let these veggies cook in their own juices since they are all moisture laden. Stir them occasionally and add salt when they are partially cooked. They must retain their bright colour and spongy texture. Just before taking off the flame add the powdered peanuts and mix in till all the vegetables are well-coated. Transfer to a serving dish and garnish with chopped coriander.

Serve hot with rotis or parathas.

Opposite: Baby Boom – with baby onions, brinjals and tomatoes

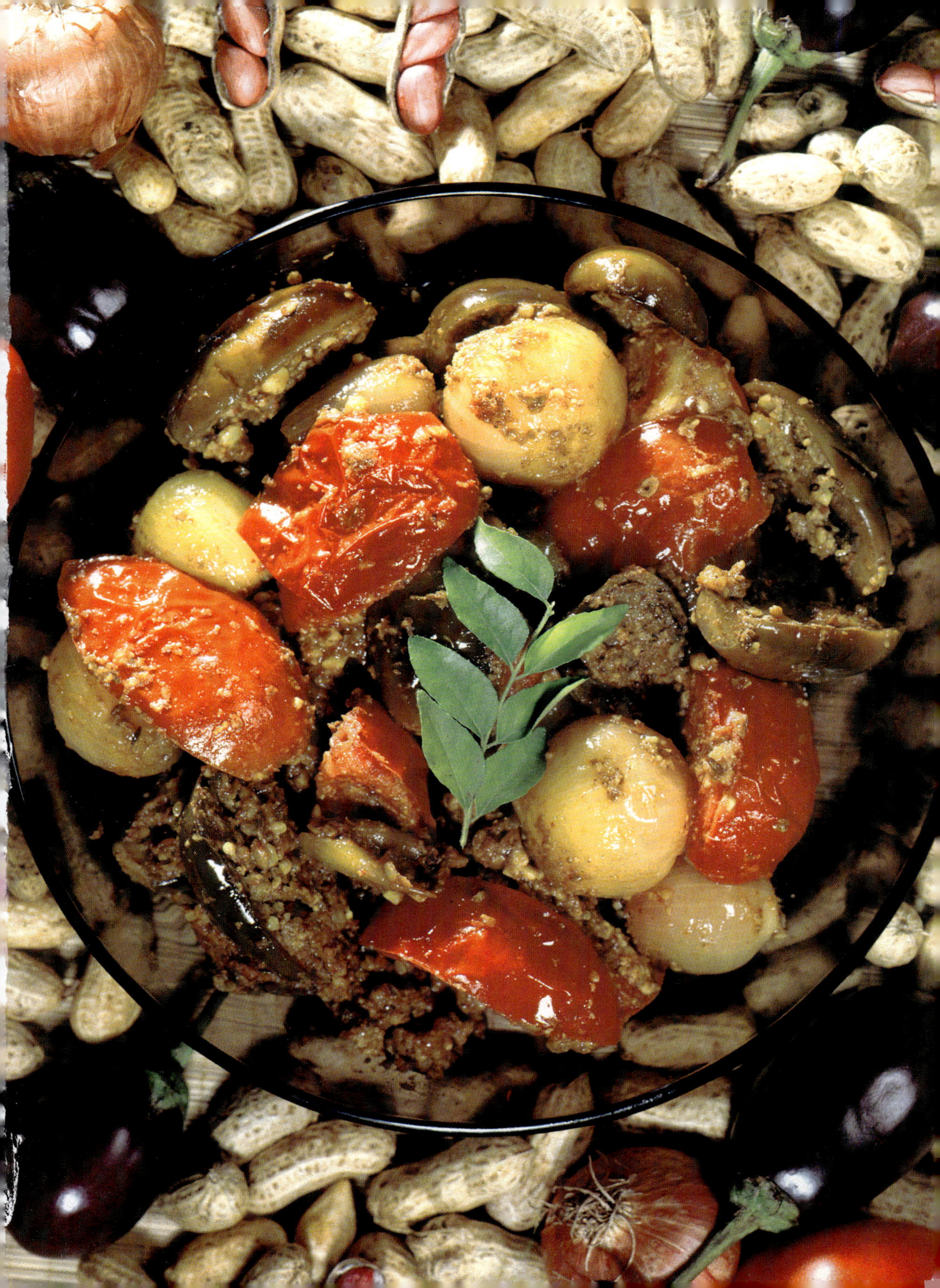

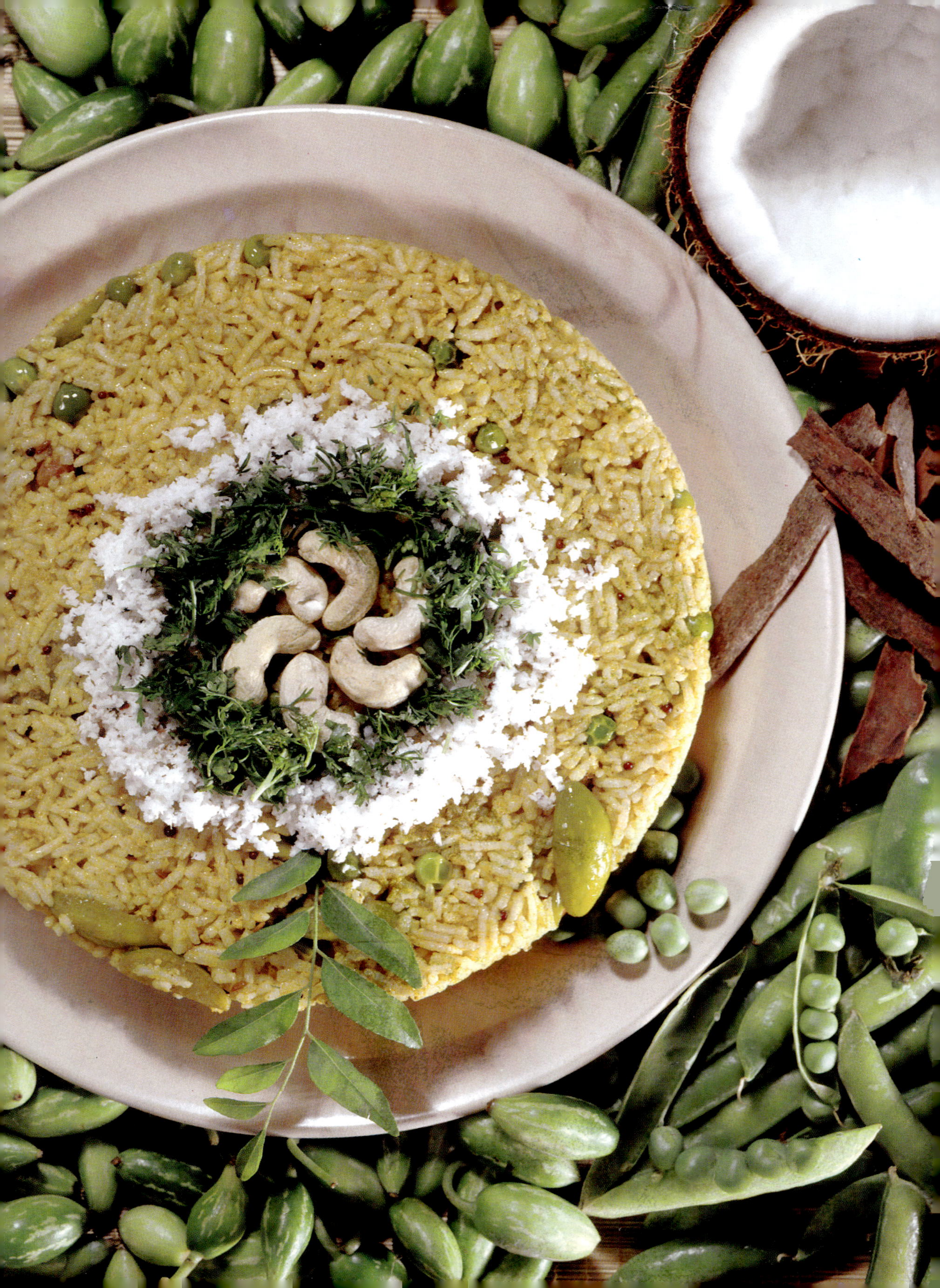

Serves 4-6

Spinach Kheema

This is a vegetarian dish that gives a whiff of the strong flavours of meat. The secret ingredient is the soya nuggets. These are a delicious way to consume this high-protein seed and since they come pre-prepared they are easy to use as well. While they retain as much protein content as meat, the quality of this is easily assimilated and the flavour is meaty too.

Ingredients

Spinach	1 bunch
Soya nuggets	1½ cups
Ginger garlic paste	2 tbsp
Onion, chopped	1 large
Chilles, chopped	2 green
Red chillie powder or to taste	1 tsp
Coriander powder	2 tbsp
Cumin powder	1 tbsp
Garam masala	1 tsp
Turmeric powder	1 tsp
Asafoetida	¼ tsp
Cumin seeds	1 tsp
Oil of your choice	2 tsp
Salt to taste	
Lime, juiced	1
Tofu or cottage cheese for garnish	2 tbsp

Opposite: Masala Bhaat – with tondli and peas (refer page 85)

Method

Clean and wash the spinach thoroughly. Chop the spinach. Soak the soya nuggets in hot water for 15 minutes. Drain water and break the nuggets into smaller pieces if desired.

Heat oil in a thick bottomed pan and place the cumin seeds in it. When the cumin starts to move around add the turmeric and asafoetida powders and sauté for 30 seconds. Then add the onions and sauté till translucent. Then add the ginger-garlic paste and green chillies and sauté for a minute. Next add the chopped spinach, soya nuggets, the coriander and cumin powders and enough water to cook the spinach. Cook with pan covered. Cook till almost done and then add the salt. Sprinkle the garam masala powder just before taking the pan off the flame. Keep covered for 5 minutes to let the aroma infuse with the vegetable. Add the lime juice to the mixture, and mash it thoroughly. Garnish with crumbled tofu or cottage cheese and serve hot with rotis or rice.

Serves 4-6

Capsicum Delight

Capsicum is one of those demanding vegetables that cannot be ignored after being put in the pan. Cook too long and it will look like a ghost of it's vibrant self. Leave it without stirring and the bottom gets overdone while the top is left uncooked. So if you are cooking this vegetable make sure you are all there. Take the phone off the hook if you like.

Ingredients

Green capsicum, deseeded and cubed	350 gms
Roasted split chickpeas, powdered	½ cup
Grated or dehydrated coconut	½ cup
Red chillie powder	1 tsp
Mustard seeds	1 tsp
Turmeric powder	1 tsp
Asafoetida	½ tsp
Salt to taste	
Oil of your choice	2 tsp

Method

Heat the oil in a thick-bottomed pan and place the mustard in it. When the mustard begins to splutter add the turmeric powder and asafoetida and sauté for 30 seconds. Add the cubed capsicum and stir fry for a minute and add a little water for cooking the capsicum. Cook covered for not more than five minutes. The colour of the capsicum must not pale. Then add the roasted split chick pea powder, coconut, keeping aside a tablespoon for garnish, chillie powder and salt and mix the whole lot together. Add enough water so that it can blend well.

This is a well-blended moist vegetable dish, neither wet nor dry. Cook covered for a couple of minutes, stirring occasionally. Transfer to a serving dish and garnish with the remaining coconut.

Serve hot with plain rotis or parathas.

Raw Banana Curry

The fibre and iron content of the banana stays intact even when cooked. Luckily this vegetable is available throughout the year and therefore can put in an appearance at least once a week.

Ingredients

Raw bananas of any variety	5
Fresh grated coconut	1 tbsp
Chopped fresh coriander	1 tbsp

For the Seasoning

Oil of your choice	2 tsp
Mustard	
Fenugreek seeds	5–6
Turmeric powder	½ tsp
Asafoetida	¼ tsp
Curry leaves	5–6
Split black gram	1 tsp
Split Bengal gram	1 tsp

Method

Steam cook the bananas with adequate water and salt till tender but not mushy. Peel and dice them.

Heat the oil in a pan and place the mustard in it. When it splutters add the rest of the seasoning ingredients and sauté for 30 seconds. Add the diced bananas to this and sauté till the vegetable is well coated with seasoning. Check salt and add if required. Stir-fry on a low flame till banana cubes turn crisp.

Transfer to a serving bowl and garnish with the coconut and coriander and serve hot with rotis or rice.

Serves 4-6

Arbi Masala

Colocasia is another rich source of soluble fibre and iron. The starchy taste of arbi is contrasted by the tartness of tamarind, the pungent flavour of the Bishop's weed and the nutty flavour of the cumin and poppy – an ideal example of what a pinch of this and a pinch of that can do to the most ordinary vegetable.

Ingredients

Arbi	500 gms
Tamarind	1 lemon sized ball
Salt to taste	
Fresh chopped coriander	1 tbsp

For the Seasoning

Cumin seeds	2 tsp
Bishop's weed	1 tsp
Turmeric powder	1 tsp
Asafoetida	¼ tsp
Poppy seeds	1 tsp
Oil of your choice	2 tsp

Method

Cook the coclocasia in plenty of water till soft. Leave to cool, peel and slice into thick roundels. Soak the tamarind in a cup of water. Heat the oil in a thick-bottomed pan and place the cumin in it. When the cumin begins to move around, add the rest of the seasoning ingredients and sauté for 30 seconds. Add the tamarind extract and salt and bring to a boil. Finally add the sliced arbi and mix well. Cook on a low flame till the tamarind extract turns to a thick gravy. Check salt and add if required. Stir occasionally to prevent the arbi sticking to the pan.

Transfer to a serving bowl and garnish with chopped coriander and serve with rotis or rice.

Serves 4-6

Serves 4-6

Ladies Finger Just Right

Ladies Finger is known as a brain vegetable but due to its mucilaginous property it is tricky to cook. The secret is to cook it on a low flame and take it off the heat when it is turns a dark green and is cooked just right. Delay by a few seconds and it will turn brown and break up. Avoid adding any water while cooking.

Ingredients

Ladies finger	500 gms
Onion, chopped fine (optional)	1 medium
Coriander powder	1 tbsp
Cumin powder	½ tbsp
Dry mango powder	1 tsp
Pepper powder	¼ tsp
Red chilly powder	1 tsp
Coconut, grated for garnish	1 tbsp
Salt to taste	

For the Seasoning

Oil of your choice	2 tsp
Mustard seeds	1 tsp
Turmeric powder	½ tsp
Asafoetida	¼ tsp

Method

Wash the vegetable thoroughly and pat dry. Chop into half inch pieces.

Heat the oil in a thick-bottomed pan and place the mustard in it. When it begins to splutter add the rest of the seasoning ingredients and sauté for 10 seconds. Add the onions and brown. Then add the chopped ladies finger and sauté till well-coated with the seasoning. Add the dry spice powders and salt and mix well till the vegetable is well coated.

Cook uncovered and stir often so that the vegetable does not burn. Stir-fry gently on a low flame to prevent burning. In about 5 minutes it will turn a dark green. Press one piece to check whether it breaks easily to test whether it is cooked.

Take it off the flame but leave in the pan so that it cooks a little more. Transfer to serving bowl and garnish with grated coconut.

Serve with rotis or rice.

Serves 4-6

Bottle Gourd with Whole Chick Pea Sprouts

This is usually prepared with split Bengal gram but sprouts are a better substitute for nutrition and easy digestibility. This is a fortified vegetable, iron and protein enhanced, so to say, but naturally, unlike the tinned products that do so by synthetic means.

Ingredients

Bottle gourd, skinned and cubed	500 gms
Chick pea sprouts	2 cups
Onion, chopped fine	1 medium
Garlic, minced	4 cloves
Ginger, minced	2 inch piece
Dry mango powder	1 tsp
Anardana	½ tsp
Coriander powder, for garnish	1 tbsp
Salt to taste	

For the Seasoning

Cumin seeds	1 tsp
Fenugreek seeds	5-6
Turmeric powder	½ tsp
Asafoetida	¼ tsp
Oil of your choice	2 tsp

Method

Cook the sprouts till soft. Mash lightly with back of spoon. Heat the oil in a pan and place the cumin seeds in it. When they begin to move add the rest of the seasoning ingredients and sauté for 10 seconds. Add the rest of the ingredients, except the garnish, and mix well. Finally add the cooked sprouts and a little of the water used to cook them so that any nutrients are not wasted. Cook till soft. Since bottle gourd cooks fast it need not take more than 5 minutes.

Transfer to a serving bowl and garnish with chopped coriander.

Serve hot with rotis or parathas.

Aubergine Delight

Aubergine is a widely available vegetable all over the world and is adaptable to various cuisines but this is my favourite method of eating it. The Arabic tradition of eating this is by blending it with puréed cooked Bengal gram and sesame seed paste. Just goes to prove the verastility of the vegetable.

Ingredients

Brinjals	2 large
Onion, chopped fine	1 large
Dry mango powder	1 tsp
Plain yogurt, beaten	1 cup
Salt to taste	
Fresh coriander for garnish	1 tbsp

For the Seasoning

Cumin seeds	1 tsp
Fenugreek seeds	5–6
Turmeric powder	½ tsp
Asafoetida	¼ tsp
Curry leaves	5–6
Green chillies, chopped fine	2
Ginger, chopped fine	1 inch piece
Oil of your choice	2 tsp

Method

Roast the brinjals on the stove top or microwave. Leave to cool and peel off skin.

Heat the oil in a pressure pan and place the cumin seeds in it. When they begin to move add the rest of the seasoning ingredients and sauté for 10 seconds. Add the chopped onion and sauté till they turn translucent. In a big bowl mash the peeled aubergine. Add salt and the seasoning and mix well.

Transfer to a serving bowl and chill. Garnish with chopped coriander before serving.

Serve with phulkas or parathas.

Serves 4-6

RICE IS NICE

For many of us rice is our staple diet. Yet the nutritional value of the rice we currently eat bothers me. It is polished so fine that any vitamins residing in the bran are lost to us. Interestingly, the first known mention of khichri comes from a Frenchman, Jean Baptiste Tavernier, a jeweller and merchant who made six trips to India between 1640-85. He mentions that khichri made with green gram, rice, butter and salt was the popular peasant evening meal. Now with increasing nutritional awareness, some shops stock semi-polished and unpolished raw rice as well. The aroma of this rice is enough to convert you to eating it permanently. But it takes time to get used to the taste. When your taste buds are used to pasty rice, chewing on a little bran seems like a chore. But give yourself time and you will yourself notice that this rice is a lot tastier than polished rice.

There is a variety of red rice also available, which is high in soluble fibre content as also a small amount of B complex vitamins. When cooked it has a brownish tinge. This too has a rich taste but takes getting used to. While experimenting with new varieties it is prudent to go in for small quantities and try them out intermittently so that both your tongue and your mind have time to familiarise themselves with the taste, smell and colour.

Some of us may not be able to make the switch right away. It's okay. You can compensate for this by substituting broken wheat for rice, particularly in dishes like khichris. Put these on your menu once a fortnight to begin with. You may be able to bring it down to once or twice a week, later. This is in order to fortify our meals with the fibre that is actually our lifeline to good health.

Split-Lentil Rice

Serves 4-6

Some memories tug at your heart, some at your taste-buds. This dish tugs at both of them for me. It evokes pictures of huge family gatherings in almost monsoon weather when we all sat on the ground in rows facing each other and the aroma of Hooggi - as this rice dish is known in the southern state of Karnataka in India- would waft across, arousing the sweet anticipation of bliss. What small joys filled us then!

Ingredients

Rice	2 cups
Split green mung with skin	1 cup
Desiccated coconut	½ cup
Cumin seeds	1 tbsp
Cloves	5–6
Cashew nuts, whole	1 tbsp
Ghee	2 tsp
Ghee to serve	

Method

Clean, wash and soak the mung in adequate water for 15 minutes. Clean, wash and drain the rice.

Dry roast the cumin, coconut and cloves till you get a wonderful aroma. Leave to cool and dry grind them. Heat the ghee in a pressure pan and sauté the rice in it for a minute. Then add the dry masala you have freshly ground and the soaked mung. Mix the three thoroughly and add adequate water to cook the khichri. Khichris are usually on the runny side, unlike pilauos, you should therefore add a little extra water while cooking. Finally add the cashew nuts and cook till the rice is absolutely soft. Immediately after taking the lid off the pan add salt and mash the khichri well. Transfer to a serving dish with a lid. Add a generous dollop of ghee and cover the dish. You need no other garnish. Take off the lid only when you serve.

Serve piping hot with raita and roasted papad.

Serves 4-6

Cabbage Rice

You could say this is India's answer to the Chinese fried rice. Thankfully it is not fried and for good measure we have even spiced it up. You can chop the cabbage and sauté it while the rice is cooking which means it takes less than 20 minutes to prepare and get this dish to the table. Cabbage rice could qualify as a dish for all seasons.

Ingredients

Shredded cabbage	500 gms
Rice	2 cups
Onion	1 medium
Garlic, peeled and minced	2 cloves
Ginger, grated	1 inch piece
Green chillies, chopped fine (optional)	2
Pav-bhaji masala	2 tsp
Salt to taste	
Oil of your choice	2 tsp
Chopped coriander	½ cup

Method

Cook the rice and leave to cool. Meanwhile heat oil in a thick-bottomed pan and place the onions and garlic in it. Sauté till the onion turns translucent. Then add the green chillie and ginger. Sauté for 10 seconds more. Finally add the shredded cabbage and pav bhaji masala and toss to mix well. Add a sprinkling of water and cook covered for not more than 5 minutes. The cabbage should be tender but crunchy as in Chinese fried rice. Add salt, mix well and take off the flame.

Mix in the cooked rice, check the salt and add more if required. Reheat, if you wish, on a low flame. Transfer to a serving plate and garnish with chopped coriander and ginger juliennes.

Rice Dhokla

Serves 4-6

The traditional dhokla is made with chickpea flour which many people find a little heavy for digestion. Millet or bajra, on the other hand, is far easier. Among the cereals it is also least acid-genic and could therefore be happily had by people with a tendency to develop acidity after a heavy meal. Bajra will however impart a brownish tinge to the dhokla and therefore the use of turmeric powder to liven up the appearance.

Ingredients

Rice, soaked for 4 hours	2 cups
Millet flour	1 cup
Green chillies	4–5
Ginger	2 inch piece
Chopped mixed vegetables (carrot, beans, peas, corn)	3 cups
Sour yogurt	1 cup
Turmeric powder	½ tsp
Salt to taste	
Oil for greasing pan	
Chopped coriander	1 tbsp
Grated coconut	1 tbsp

Method

Grind the soaked rice to a coarse paste. Add the ginger and green chillies and grind once more. Mix in the millet flour in small quantities at a time along with the sour yogurt and turmeric powder and blend well, adding water if necessary. Add the chopped mixed vegetables and salt and mix well. The batter should be of dropping consistency like idli batter.

Grease a pan and steam the batter for 15–20 minutes as you do for idlis. Cut into square or rectangular dhoklas, as you please.

Transfer to a serving plate, garnish with the chopped coriander and serve hot with a mint or any other green chutney.

Note 1: Any leftovers can be sautéed in a seasoning of mustard and asafoetida and served with tomato ketchup.

Note 2: You can substitute idli rava for rice. You don't need to soak the rava before grinding. But preparing the batter, without the vegetables, and leaving it out for 4 hours will make it rise a little and also turn out lighter dhoklas. The vegetables can be added just before preparing the dhoklas.

Serves 4-6

Basbhatta

This is a variation on a Kashmiri rice dish, only we are using sprouted kabuli chana or whole chick peas.

Ingredients

Basmati rice	2 cups
Whole chick pea sprouts	2 cups
Onions, diced	2 medium
Ginger, minced	2 inch piece
Garlic, minced	4 cloves
Amchur	½ tsp
Anardana	¼ tsp
Oil of your choice	1 tbsp

Whole Masala

Bay leaf	1
Cloves	4
Peppercorn	1 tsp
Cardamom, split	1 big

Method

Wash the rice, drain and set aside for 15 minutes.

Heat the oil in a pan and add the whole masalas. Sauté for 30 seconds till you get a rich aroma. Then add the onions and sauté till they turn translucent. Add ginger and garlic and sauté for 30 seconds more. Finally add the rice and sauté till it is well coated with oil. Add 5 cups of water to this, along with the sprouted kabuli chana (chick peas) and salt. Cover the pan and cook for 10 minutes or till the chick peas are soft. Sprouted whole grain generally takes less time to cook.

Serve hot with roasted papad and raita.

Saffron Rice

This is a sweet variety of rice. This could be part of a festive meal and goes as the main course. Saffron has blood-purifying qualities and inclusion of this condiment in our diet is very therapeutic.

Ingredients

Rice	2 cups
Jaggery, sliced	1 cup
Coconut milk	2 cups
Cardamom, crushed	¼ tsp
Saffron strands	1 tsp
Cloves	4
Ghee	2 tsp
Milk	1 tbsp

Method

Clean, wash and drain rice. Heat ghee in a thick-bottomed deep pan and sauté the cloves for 10 seconds. Add the rice and sauté till the grains turn translucent. Pour in the coconut milk and 3 cups of water and cook on a low flame, stirring occasionally.

In another thick-bottomed pan melt the jaggery by heating on a low flame and stirring continuously to prevent burning. Take off the flame immediately after it melts, do not let it turn into a thick syrup.

Heat the milk and pour it on the saffron strands. Rub with the back of a spoon to extract the essence. When the rice is almost cooked add the melted jaggery and the saffron to it. Check if extra water is needed. The cooked rice should come out moist but not sticky or lumpy. Cover the pan with aluminium cooking foil. Place this pan over a griddle on a low flame. Cook for about 10 minutes. This should be decided on the basis of the water left in the rice. Uncover the pan just before you serve.

Garnish with slivered almonds and serve hot.

Serves 4-6

Corn Biryani

Corn lends itself to various kinds of cuisine. But in this dish it gets to play the lead role. Tender corn is popular for its inherent sweetness, hence the term sweet corn. Early American settlements were based around the cultivation of this crop and you could say that this was also instrumental in developing civilisations in Mexico and Central America. So when you make this biryani, feel good that you are connecting to one of the world's earliest civilisations.

Ingredients

Basmati rice	2 cups
Cooked corn niblets, fresh or frozen	3 cups
Sour yogurt	1 cup
Oil of your choice	1 tbsp
Garam masala	1 tsp
Salt to taste	
Ginger juliennes for garnish	1 tbsp
Chopped coriander for garnish	1 tbsp

Dry Whole Masalas

Bay leaf	1
Cloves	4
Peppercorns	1 tsp
Cardamom, slit	1 big

To be Ground to a Paste

Onions, boiled	2 medium
Grated coconut (optional)	½ cup
Ginger	2 inch piece
Cloves garlic	4
Green chillie	1
Aniseed	1 tsp
Poppy seeds	1 tsp

Method

Clean, wash and drain rice. Set aside for 15 minutes. Cook with a teaspoon of oil so that the grains remain separate. Grind the onions and other listed ingredients to a paste and set aside. Heat the oil in a frying pan, and sauté the dry masalas for 10 seconds. Then add the onion paste and sauté till it turns brown. Add the sour yogurt, salt and boiled corn and blend well with the paste. Add a little water or even soup stock if the paste is too thick. It should be of a thick gravy consistency. In a cook-and-sserve deep pan place a thick layer of rice. Spread a thick layer of corn masala paste on top and sprinkle the garam masala. Repeat the process till all the rice and the corn masala is used up. Cover the pan with aluminum foil. Place a griddle on a low flame and place this pan on the griddle. This is the modern way of dum cooking. Cook for 10 minutes. Uncover the pan just before serving and garnish with ginger juliennes and coriander. Serve with roasted papad and raita or plain yoghurt.

Mixed Vegetable Pulao

Serves 4-6

One generally comes up with this when one runs out of ideas. At least that is the case with me. But it is still possible to add a unique touch to it, even if it is only in the garnish or the accompaniment.

Ingredients

Basmati rice	2 cups
Onion, thinly sliced	1
Cubed mixed vegetables, boiled	2 cups
Ginger, chopped fine	1 inch piece
Garlic, minced	4 cloves
Green chillies, slit vertically and deseeded	2
Cumin seeds	1 tbsp
Coriander seeds	1 tsp
Bay leaf	1
Aniseed	1 tsp
Cardamom	1 big
Cloves	4
Whole peppercorns	1 tsp
Garam masala	1 tsp
Oil	1 tbsp
Salt to taste	
Green capsicum, deseeded and cut in strips	1
Red tomato, cut in a flower shape	1

Method

Clean, wash and drain rice. Cook the rice with a drop of oil so that the grains remain separate. Heat the oil in a thick-bottomed pan and place the dry spices in it. Sauté for 30 seconds and then add the onion to it. Sauté till it turns translucent and then add the green chillie, ginger and garlic and sauté for 10 seconds. Add the boiled vegetables and salt and sauté for two minutes till they are coated with the essence of the dry spices. Finally mix in the cooked rice gently, so as to keep the grains intact. Add salt if required and blend well. Transfer to a serving plate.

To cut the tomato into a flower, insert a sharp knife in the centre and carve round the circumference as if you were sculpting a mountain range. When you reach the starting point twist the knife through the inside of the tomato and separate the two halves. Scoop out the seeds. Place in the middle of the pulao to look like a flower. Use the green capsicum to resemble stem and leaves.

Kaya Ganji

There are days when you crave for certain mild and subtle flavours. Try this dish on those days. I would describe it as a healing food. It fills you up with warmth and peace like grandma's quilt. Coconut milk on its own is a great healer too.

Ingredients

Rice (brown)	2 cups
Coconut milk	3 cups
Ghee	1 tsp
Cumin seeds	1 tsp
Cloves	1 tsp
Cinnamon	1 inch piece
Salt to taste	

Method

Clean, wash and drain the rice. Prepare the coconut milk by extracting juice from fresh grated coconut or using ready mix coconut milk powder. Heat the ghee in a pressure pan and place all the dry spices in it. Sauté till the aroma engulfs the kitchen. Add the rice to it and sauté till the grains look translucent.

Pour in the coconut milk and add 3 cups of water and cook uncovered. Add extra water if required. This rice tastes better if slightly overcooked and soft. When the rice is almost done add the salt. Stir occasionally to prevent burning and cook throughout on a low flame.

Now you know why this is a healing food; because of all the dedication that goes into preparing it.

Serves 4-6

Sesame Rice

Serves 4-6

Sesame is a rich source of calcium and this dish is a tasty way of incorporating it in the menu. The other good thing about this item is that it tastes good served cold and can be made ahead of time. Try it for your next party meal.

Ingredients

Rice	2 cups
Sesame, unpolished	¾ cup
Salt to taste	
Lime, juiced	1

For the Seasoning

Ghee	2 tsp
Mustard	1 tsp
Asafoetida	¼ tsp
Black gram dal	1 tsp
Bengal gram	1 tsp
Dry red chillies	5–6
Curry leaves	½ cup

Method

Cook rice with a drop of oil so that the grains remain separate even after cooking. Bring to room temperature. Then spread out in a large plate to cool off. Dry roast the sesame and powder it.

Prepare a seasoning by heating the ghee and placing the mustard in it. When the mustard splutters add the rest of the seasoning ingredients to it and sauté for 30 seconds. Sprinkle salt and sesame powder over the cooled rice. Pour the seasoning over it and mix well with a spatula. Finally add the lime juice and mix once more.

Grease a jelly mould lightly and prepare a mould of this rice. Unmould it onto a pretty china rice plate just before serving. Serve with a yogurt based salad and papads.

Serves 4-6

Masala Bhaat

Some vegetables like tendli are not the most favourite with some of us. This dish is an excellent way to consume them for their nutrition. The rich spices do a total makeover of the vegetable.

Ingredients

Rice	2 cups
Tendli, sliced lengthwise	400 gms
Green peas	1 cup
Grated coconut	½ cup
Plain yogurt	1 cup
Coriander powder	1 tbsp
Garam masala	2 tsp
Or substitute the above two with goda masala	1 tbsp
Red chillie powder	1 tsp
Green chillie, slit lengthwise and deseeded	1

For the Seasoning

Oil of your choice	1 tbsp
Mustard seeds	1 tsp
Turmeric powder	½ tsp
Asafoetida	¼ tsp
Curry leaves	1 tbsp
Chopped cashew nuts	1 tbsp

Method

Clean, wash and drain the rice. In a pressure pan heat the oil and place the mustard. When it splutters add the rest of the seasoning ingredients and sauté for 30 seconds. Add the sliced tendli and sauté till they are well coated with oil. Mix in the yogurt, salt, spices and rice. Add enough water to cook the rice and vegetables taking the moisture of the yogurt into account. Cook for required amount of time.

Transfer to serving bowl and garnish with the slit green chillie in the centre and the coconut around it. Surround the coconut with chopped coriander.

Serve piping hot with kadhi lajawaab.

Green Mango Rice

Serves 4-6

Raw mangoes are rich in ascorbic acid and so are important for good health. This tangy rice can be made ahead of time. It is great for the summer months when you don't really want to eat steaming hot meals. Nature has it reasons for bringing us seasonal vegetables and fruits.

Ingredients

Rice	2 cups
Tart green mangoes	2 medium
Salt to taste	
Chopped fresh coriander	1 tbsp

For the Seasoning

Oil of your choice	1 tbsp
Mustard seeds	1 tsp
Fenugreek seeds	5–6
Turmeric powder	½ tsp
Asafoetida	¼ tsp
Dry red chillies	2–3
Black gram	1 tsp
Bengal gram	1 tsp
Curry leaves	5–6

Method

Cook the rice with a drop of oil so that the grains remain separate. Bring to room temperature and spread on a large plate to cool.

Peel the mangoes and grate them.

Heat the oil in a pan and place the mustard in it. When the mustard splutters add the rest of the seasoning ingredients and sauté for 30 seconds. Sprinkle salt and the grated mango over the cooled rice and mix well. Pour the seasoning over this and mix again.

Transfer to a serving dish and garnish with chopped coriander. Serve with a cucumber – split mung salad for a balanced meal.

BREAD BASKET

The variety of breads available is really amazing. The roti, naans, parathas and even the Arabic khuboos – similar to our tandoori roti only much thicker and softer, the Turkish lavash similar to rumali roti, the Iranian markook also like the rumali roti but layered. The moulded breads, many of them available at the corner shops in most Indian metros, offer a wide variety like brown, wholemeal, rye, multigrain, French stick, too. Bread is healthy and has a high fibre content, is rich in iron and vitamins, especially the B complex group and is also a valuable source of calcium. Mass produced bread contains additives, including fat, preservatives, salt and emulsifiers. Salt is added for flavour and to strngthen the gluten which is what makes the dough malleable. But the thing to remember is that the milling process determines the food value of the bread and the milling process determines the type of flour. Comercially available wheat flour is usually refined and sometimes bleached though none of this is mentioned on the label. In the process the germ and bran are removed. It is best to use wholemeal flour milled at your neighbourhood flour mill. Maida or plain flour or white flour used in all cake, biscuit and most bread recipes is devoid of either germ or bran. Soya flour, from soya beans, which is 20 per cent fat and 34 per cent protein, comparable to that available from meat and more easily absorbed at that, retains most of the original nutrients, notably the B-complex, E, phosphorous, calcium and iron. You can replace up to 20 per cent of wheat flour used to make chapattis with soya flour or add soya beans to the wheat when you get it milled.

Hi-energy Parathas

Serves 4-6

There are times when you want to have a substantial and nourishing meal but cannot go in for elaborate menus. That's the time to roll out stuffed parathas. Potatoes have a high glyceamic index and are not for those wanting to maintain ideal body weight. But of course any food in moderation adds variety to life. So we have included the potato as one of the ingredients in a well-balanced paratha.

Ingredients

Whole wheat flour	3 cups
Chopped spinach	1 cup
Potato, boiled and mashed	1 medium
Green chillies, deseeded and chopped fine	2
Dry mango powder	1 tsp
Red chillie powder	½ tsp
Coriander powder	1 tsp
Cumin powder	1 tsp
Salt to taste	
Oil	2 tsp

Method

Place all the ingredients, except the oil, together in a large bowl and mix well, without adding any water. When they are well mixed, knead into a thick dough by adding a little water at a time. Finally add the oil and knead till the dough absorbs it. Set aside for 15 minutes.

Roll out slightly thick parathas and dry roast them on both sides on a hot griddle. Serve hot with a bowl of plain yogurt and a salad.

Note: You can substitute the spinach with fenugreek leaves and that will taste great too.

Serves 4-6

Stuffed Cauliflower Parathas

Millet flour provides high-quality protein, a wide range of B vitamins, calcium, potassium and particularly iron. Combined with wheat it gives a wonderful flavour, colour and texture.

Ingredients

For the Filling

Cauliflower, washed and grated	250 gms
Finely chopped fresh coriander	1 tbsp
Green chillies, deseeded and chopped fine	2–3
Coriander powder	1 tsp
Salt to taste	

For the Dough

Whole wheat flour	3 cups
Millet flour	½ cup
Oil	2 tsp

Method

Clean, wash thoroughly and grate the cauliflower. Sprinkle salt on it and set aside for 15 minutes. Then squeeze out the water from the cauliflower and set aside for kneading the dough. Add the rest of the stuffing ingredients and mix well. Use the cauliflower water to prepare the dough. Since this will already have salt content from the salt sprinkled on the grated cauliflower, there is no need to add extra salt. Use more water, if required. Knead a moderately soft dough. Add the oil and knead till the dough absorbs it. Set aside for 15 minutes.

Divide the dough into small balls. Roll out 2 discs of 2 inch diameter. Spread a teaspoon of the filling on one disc and place the other disc on top of it. Seal the edges by pressing between the thumb and pointer finger. Roll out again to make a thick paratha.

Heat a griddle and dry roast the paratha on both sides. Repeat the whole process till the filling is used up.

Serve hot with baigan bharta and a salad.

Mooli Parathas

Serves 4-6

The aroma of a mooli paratha roasting is enough to have your gastric juices flowing. On a crisp winter morning in the Punjab you will find your nose leading you to this appetising aroma at every streetside dhaba. Served with a bowl of yougurt you are armed with all the energy you need for the rest of the day. If you are looking for a brunch, here's your answer.

Ingredients

Radish, washed and grated	1 medium
Whole wheat flour	3 cups
Celery seeds	1 tsp
Onion seeds	1 tsp
Finely chopped fresh coriander	1 tbsp
Green chillies, deseeded and chopped fine	3
Ginger, grated	1 inch piece
Salt to taste	

Method

Mix all the ingredients together and knead well without adding any water in the beginning. The moisture in the radish will be enough to bind the dough but if it is inadequate add as required.

Roll out into parathas immediately or the dough will start becoming loose with the radish-salt combination secreting moisture. Dry roast on both sides.

Serve hot with a yogurt salad.

Serves 4-6

Tofu Parathas

With fresh tofu so easily available in the market, it is tempting to try these parathas. They are just as rich and smooth as the dairy cottage cheese ones. If tofu is not available, you can substitute it with low-fat dairy cottage cheese.

Ingredients

For the Filling

Tofu	2 cups
Finely chopped fresh coriander	1 tbsp
Dry mango powder	1 tsp
Coriander powder	1 tsp
Cumin powder	1 tsp
Salt to taste	
Green chillies, deseeded and chopped fine	3
Red chillie powder	½ tsp

For the Dough

Whole wheat flour	4 cups
Salt to taste	
Oil	2 tsp

Method

Crumble the tofu or cottage cheese and mix in the rest of the filling ingredients. Mix well to form a dry thick filling. If you feel that the tofu or cottage cheese has more water, wrap in a clean muslin cloth, place in a colander and put a heavy griddle or any other weight on top to drain the water. Then carry on as above.

Meanwhile knead the flour with water and salt to make a medium soft dough. Let it sit for 15 minutes.

Divide the dough into small balls. Fashion a cup with the ball and put in 1 teaspoon of the filling. Pinch the edges together to seal and roll it around between your palms to shape into a ball again. Roll out thick parathas and dry roast both sides on a hot griddle.

Serve hot with a kadhi and plain salad.

Sprout Parathas

Serves 4-6

For those of us who are not very fond of sprouts in their raw form, the sprout paratha is a good beginning. It transforms into a creamy stuffing, which, with added spices is very, very tasty. It is also another way of recycling any leftover sprouts.

Ingredients

For the Filling

Mung sprouts, boiled and mashed	1 cup
Red mung or matki sprouts, boiled and mashed	1 cup
Finely chopped fresh coriander	2 tbsp
Dry mango powder	1 tsp
Green chilies, deseeded and chopped fine	3-4
Red chillie powder	½ tsp
Salt to taste	

For the Dough

Whole wheat flour	4 cups
Salt to taste	
Oil	2 tsp

Method

Cook the sprouts till absolutely dry. Mash well and add the rest of the filling ingredients and mix well to make a thick dry filling.

Knead the flour with water and salt to make a medium soft dough. Keep for 15 minutes.

Divide the dough into small balls. Fashion a cup with the ball and put in 1 teaspoon of the filling. Pinch the edges together to seal and roll it around between your palms to shape into a ball again. Roll out thick parathas and dry roast on both sides on a hot griddle.

Serve hot with yogurt salad and a green chutney.

Opposite: Sprout Parathas

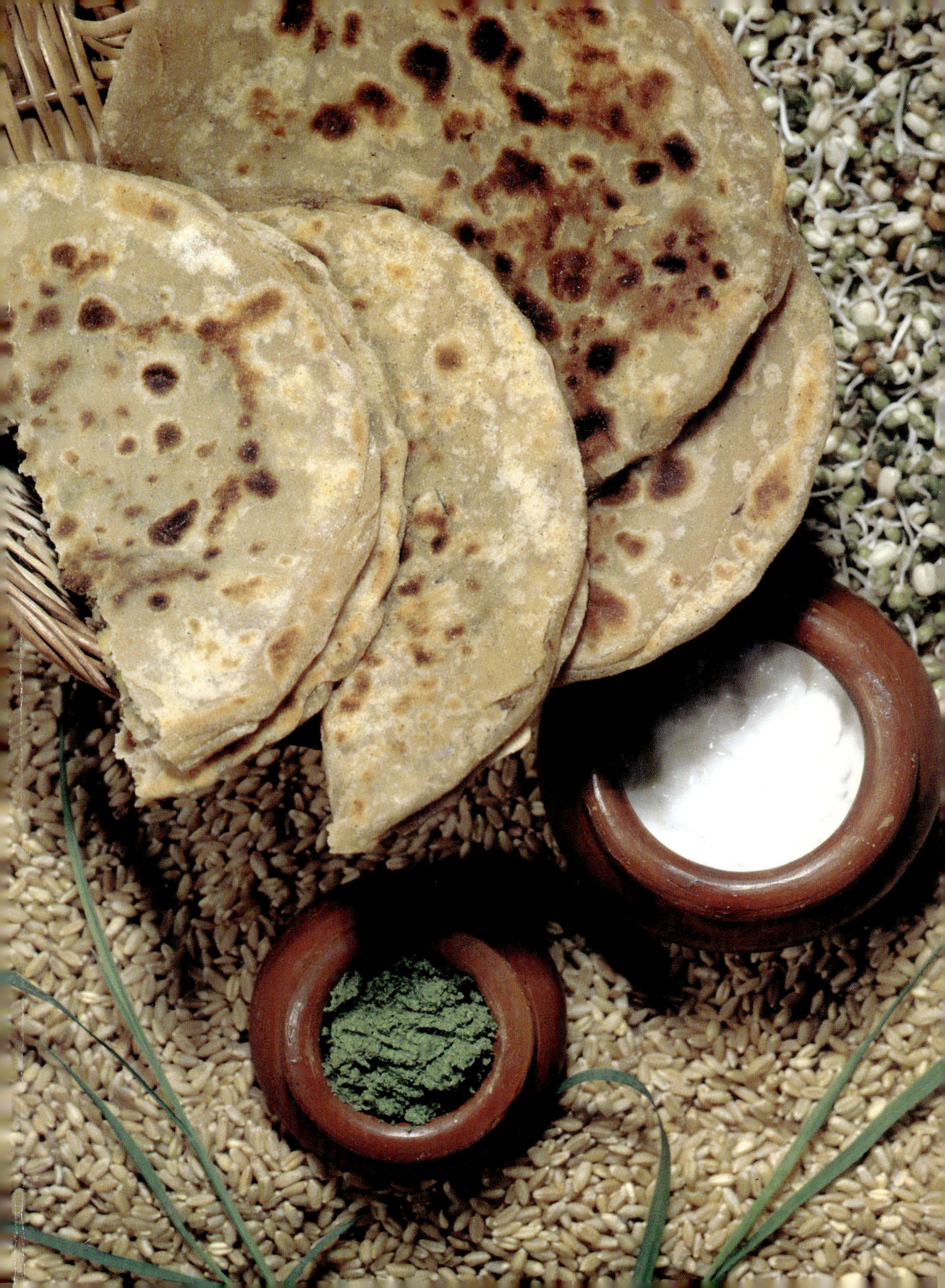

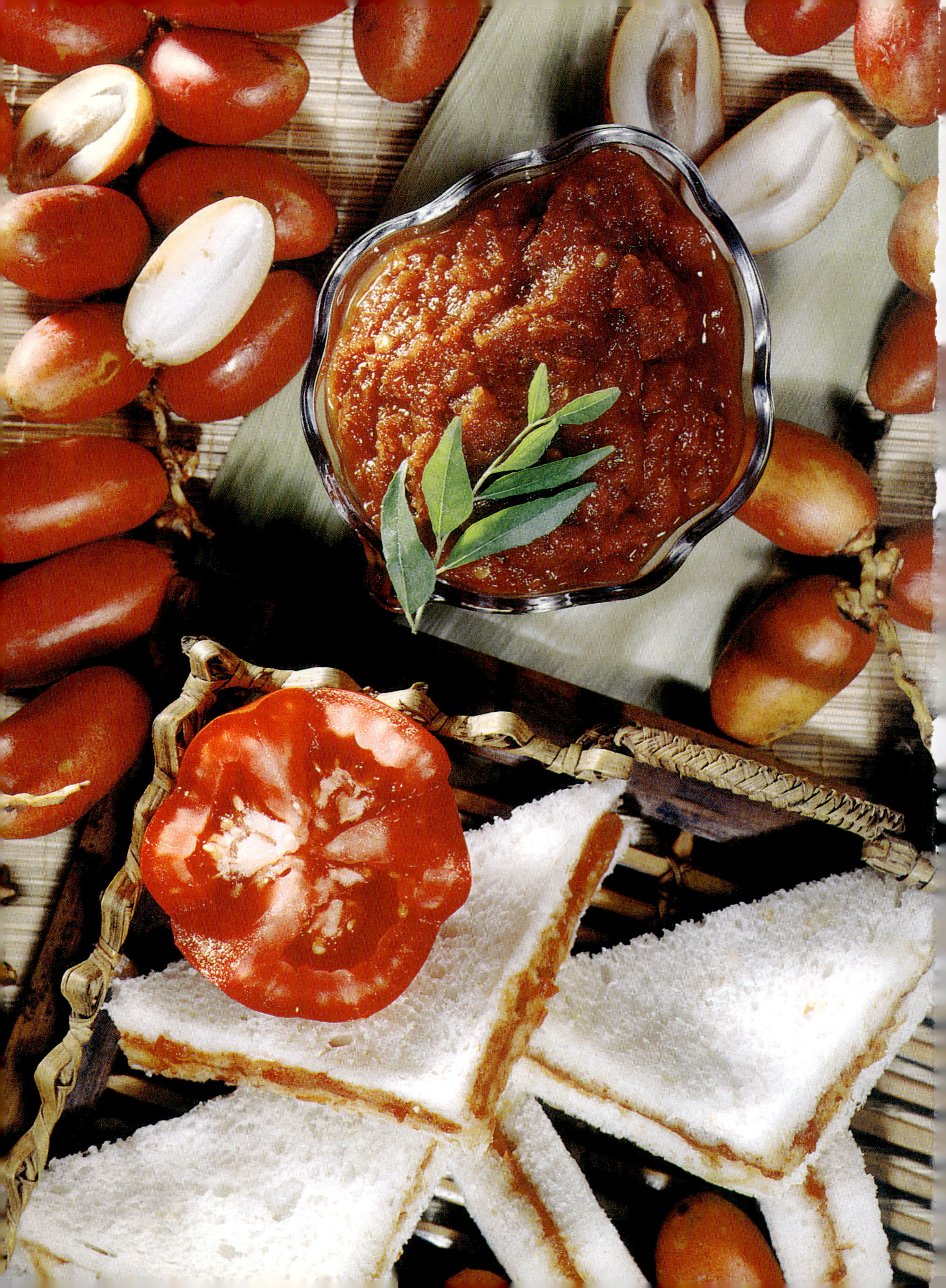

Serves 4-6

Cabbage Parathas

The cabbage, it appears, is a versatile vegetable. It can be used in a variety of dishes combined with rice, wheat flour, semolina and of course by itself in a curry. Here is a tasty version in paratha form.

Ingredients

Grated cabbage or shredded fine	3 cups
Whole wheat flour	3 cups
Finely chopped fresh coriander	1 tbsp
Ginger, grated	1 inch
Green chillies, deseeded and chopped fine	3
Red chillie powder	½ tsp
Salt to taste	
Oil	2 tsp

Method

Put together all the ingredients, except the oil, in a large bowl and knead well without adding any water in the beginning. The dough should be thick so add only as much water as is required later. Roll out medium thick parathas immediately or else the cabbage-salt combination will make the dough watery. Dry roast both sides on a hot griddle.

Serve hot with a yogurt-sprout salad and a chutney.

Opposite: Tomato – Date Sandwich Spread (ref. page 116)

Peas Parathas

Serves 4-6

Peas have an interesting history. The earliest mention seems to be in the Yajurveda, where it merits a mention as being harvested in spring. In about 350 BC pea soup was very popular. But the peas paratha has existed since the time of Ibn Battuta, an Arabic traveller, who was received at the court of Mohammed bin Tughlak. Ibn Battuta mentions that he was captured by theives and given a bread of peas to eat.

Ingredients

For the Filling

Peas, boiled	2 cups
Finely chopped fresh coriander	1 tbsp
Green chillies, deseeded and chopped fine	2–3
Coriander powder	1 tsp
Salt to taste	

For the Dough

Whole wheat flour	3 cups
Oil	2 tsp
Salt to taste	

Method

Boil the peas and drain them of any water. Mash well immediately after boiling or grind to a coarse paste without adding any water. Add the rest of the filling ingredients and prepare a dry filling.

Divide the dough into small balls. Roll out 2 discs of 2 inch diameter. Spread a teaspoon of the filling on one disc and place the other disc on top of it. Seal the edges by pressing between your thumb and pointer finger. Roll out again to make a thick paratha. Heat a griddle and dry roast the paratha on both sides.

Serve hot with yogurt salad and sliced onions.

Ragi Rotis

There is nothing to beat this farmer's bread. It improves on acquaintance, both in preparation and taste. But it is a highly nutritive meal in itself due to the high iron and calcium content of rye.

Ingredients

Rye flour	2 cups
Rice flour	½ cup
Grated fresh coconut	1 cup
Onion, chopped fine	½ cup
Fresh coriander, chopped fine	1 tbsp
Green chilies, chopped fine	3
Salt to taste	
Oil	1 tbsp

Method

Mix all the ingredients in a large bowl. Knead to form a thick dough. Add water only if required.

Divide the dough into small balls. Grease some kitchen paper with a few drops of oil. Place the ball in the centre of the paper and with your fingers moistened with water pat the dough to flatten it. Pat the ball into as thin a roti as possible without breaking it. Moisten your fingers as often as you wish without thinning the dough too much. In the beginning your ragi rotis will turn out a little thick, but with practice they'll start getting thinner. Believe me, this dish is well worth the effort. And you'll pick up speed as you go along.

Heat a griddle and place the roti on this with the paper facing you. Peel off the paper gently once the side on the griddle begins to bake. Drizzle a few drops of oil around the roti. Bake on both sides.

Meanwhile grease another piece of kitchen paper and repeat the process. Using 2 kitchen papers repeat the process till all the dough is used up.

Serve hot with a dab of homemade butter or plain yogurt and a thin lentil soup.

Thalipeeth

Serves 4-6

This Indian flatbread comes as close to a balanced meal as a single dish can. It benefits from the mixture of the three grains and a pulse. But don't quibble too much about its food value because you'll end up liking the dish for itself - taste and aroma alike.

Ingredients

Millet flour	2 cups
Whole wheat flour	½ cup
Rice flour	½ cup
Chick pea flour	¼ cup
Cumin powder	1 tsp
Red chillie powder	2–3 tsp
grated onion	1 cup
Celery seeds	1 tsp
Fresh coriander (finely chopped)	1 tbsp
Salt to taste	
Oil of your choice	1 tbsp

Method

Place all the ingredients, except the oil, in a large bowl. Knead well without adding any water. The dough has to be thick.

Divide the dough into small balls. Grease a piece of kitchen paper with a few drops of oil. Place the ball in the centre of the paper and with your fingers moistened with water pat the dough to flatten it. Pat the ball into as thin a roti as possible without breaking it. Moisten your fingers as often as you wish without thinning the dough too much. In the beginning your thalipeeth will turn out a little thick, but with practise they will start getting thinner. This roti is so tasty that you might end up making extra dough. And you'll pick up speed as you go.

Heat a griddle and place the roti on this with the paper facing you. Peel off the paper gently once the side on the griddle begins to bake. Drizzle a few drops of oil around the roti and in the centre after pricking it lightly with a fork. Bake on both sides.

Meanwhile grease another piece of kitchen paper and repeat the process. Using 2 kitchen papers repeat the process till all the dough is used up.

Serve hot with a dab of homemade butter or plain yogurt and a salad.

Serves 4-6

Raw Banana Parathas

While the spud is not very welcome on the menu the raw banana, similar in taste, is more than welcome due to its high soluble fibre content as also the calcium it retains.

Ingredients

Raw bananas, steamed	3
Fresh coriander, chopped fine	1 tbsp
Dry mango powder	1 tsp
Coriander powder	1 tsp
Cumin powder	1 tsp
Salt to taste	
Green chillies, deseeded and chopped fine	3
Red chillie powder	½ tsp

For the Dough

Whole wheat flour	4 cups
Sour yogurt, optional	1 cup
Salt to taste	
Oil	2 tsp

Method

Steam the bananas in their skins. Leave to cool and peel. Mash well or grate and mix in the other ingredients for the filling. Bind well to form a thick dry filling.

Knead the flour with the sour yogurt and salt. Add water, if required, to make a medium soft dough. Keep for 15 minutes.

Divide the dough into small balls. Fashion a cup with the ball and put in 1 teaspoon of the filling. Pinch the edges together to seal and roll it around between your palms to shape into a ball again. Roll out thick parathas and dry roast both sides on a hot griddle.

Serve hot with a kadhi and plain salad.

TEA WITH ME

Fast food or fasting food you'll find both here. Because, come to think of it the evening tea ceremony is a disappearing tradition today. Everyone from the grand-parents down to the tiny tots are busy from dawn to dusk with enriching their lives. Add to that the mass mental meter that ticks away calories as they are consumed. And what you have is the evening tea as a first casualty to modern life. Still there are plenty of occasions — weekends, guests for high tea, a hungry stomach…which necessitate the instant appearance of a fulfilling snack without much ado. It is for times such as these that this section is designed. Some of these items double as lunch-box snacks for the kids or even to take to work. If you are in the habit of having a light breakfast you'll find something here too. For most items preparations can be made ahead and the cooking can be done as and when required. For certain others you only need have a well-stocked larder. For a few, not even that. How? Read on…

Surprise Visit

It's just one of those days when you've run out of all of your stocks and are too rushed to go out and get replenishments. It is always on one such day that your relatives will decide to drop by. Naturally. Don't panic! Just put together everything that you have in the flour department, add some imaginative seasonings and serve it with, a generous dab of your charm.

Ingredients

Rice flour	1 cup
Rye flour	1 cup
Chick pea flour	1 cup
Wheat flour	1 cup
Jowar flour or corn flour	1 cup
Yogurt, beaten	1 cup
Bishops weed	1 tsp
Cumin	1 tsp
Fresh coriander, chopped fine	1 tbsp
Green chilies, chopped fine	2
Or to taste,	
Salt to taste	
Oil (optional)	1 tbsp
Homemade butter (optional)	100 gms

Method

Mix all the flour together in a large bowl and add 4 cups of water. Beat well. Keep adding water, a little at a time, to get a dropping consistency. Make sure no lumps remain. Add the rest of the ingredients and mix well again. Check the taste, adjust seasoning and if you have the time leave this batter in the sun or in any warm corner of your kitchen for 15 minutes. If you are pressed for time you can go right ahead and prepare the dosas.

Heat a griddle. To check whether it is hot enough splash a few drops of water on it. If the griddle hisses it is ready. If not, wait for a couple of minutes more and repeat. Drop a ladleful of the batter on the hot griddle and using the back of the ladle spread the batter as thin as possible in a circular motion so that you have a nice and round dosa. If you are using a non-stick griddle you will not need any oil. But if not, you will need to drizzle a few drops of oil around the edges and the centre of the dosa. Turn over the dosa when you find the edges browned and it slips easily onto the spatula. When still hot dot with a blob of homemade butter. Serve with any dry chutney powder mixed in yogurt.

Serves 4-6

Frankly Yumm

This makes a great lunch-box snack on days when you wake up to a disorganised day and are worrying about Junior's no-holds barred comments on your state of affairs. But watch how you turn this into a win-win situation. Stephen Covey would be proud of you.

Ingredients

Home-made chapattis	2
Gongura (sorrel) chutney	2 tsp
Cheese singles of whichever type	2
Or Any cheese, grated	2 tbsp
Ghee or home-made butter	1 tsp
Onion, chopped fine	1 tbsp
Tomato, chopped fine	1 tbsp
Olives, deseeded and chopped (optional)	1 tbsp

Method

Heat the griddle and lower the flame. Place the chapatti on the hot griddle. When the chapatti is warmed and slightly browned turn it over and smear half a teaspoon of the ghee. Spread half the gongura chutney, half the date chutney, half the chopped onions and half the tomatoes on one half of the chapatti. Top this with the cheese. Fold over the chapatti and roll it as tight as possible. Stick a toothpick in the centre so that it does not unfurl. Serve hot or cold with tomato ketchup.

Incidentally, these are good as picnic takeaways too. Wrap each frankie individually in foil immediately after taking off the griddle so that they remain warm and soft.

Wheat Pancakes

Any day you're bored of the roti-subji routine, try this. The main ingredient – whole wheat flour – is the same. But you are saved the trouble of kneading the dough and rolling out the rotis. Serve the wheat dosas with coriander-mint chutney and a crunchy salad (date with cabbage). And you'll have a perfectly balanced meal.

Ingredients

Whole wheat flour	2 cups
Yogurt (optional)	½ cup
Fresh coriander, chopped	1 tbsp
Cumin, whole	1 tsp
Bishops weed	1 tsp
Turmeric powder	½ tsp
Green chillie, chopped fine	1
Or Red chillie powder	1 tsp
Salt to taste	

Method

Mix the wheat flour with the yogurt and add enough water to make a batter of dropping consistency. Blend well with a whisk or an electric hand-beater. Add the rest of the ingredients and beat well. Check the salt and adjust. The batter should spread well on dropping, if it does not, add adequate water. Heat a griddle then lower the flame. Drop one ladle of the batter and using the back of the ladle spread it around in a circular motion, as thin as possible. If you are using a non-stick griddle you need not use any oil. If not then you will have to drizzle a few drops of oil round the edges and the centre. When the edges get brown and slip over the spatula easily, turn over the pancake or dosa and cook the other side as well. Repeat with the rest of the batter or until you have as many as you require.

Serves 4-6

Sweet Crêpes

An excellent addition to a quick meal when you are looking for variety. Combines very well with the wheat dosa. Ideally you could heat two griddles and make the two varieties in tandem. Consider the cooking time – a couple of minutes – for each dosa and you'll see it's possible.

Ingredients

Whole wheat flour	1 cup
Fresh coconut, grated	1 tbsp
Jaggery, sliced fine	1 cup
Cardamom, crushed	1
Ghee for cooking	

Method

Put the jaggery and one cup of water in a thick-bottomed pan and heat it. Stir till the jaggery has dissolved. Take off flame and leave to cool.

Meanwhile measure out the wheat flour and coconut. Stir this into the cooled jaggery syrup and mix well. Add the crushed cardamom and mix again. Your batter is now ready for preparation.

Heat a griddle and lower the flame. Prepare small thick dosas. Drizzle a few drops of ghee around the edges while it is cooking. Turn over and cook both sides.

Since this is a cereal based dosa it does not have the same protein levels as that of the pulse i.e. black gram or yellow gram based dosa. You can balance this out with a cabbage and split chick pea chutney.

Tomato Omelette

This is a hybrid omelette – but for once the hybrid turns out better than the original. There is no egg in the recipe and therefore it has zero cholesterol. And it is served with toasted bread just like the original one! A regular on Udupi restaurant menus too.

Ingredients

Ripe red tomatoes	6 medium
Chick pea flour	2 cups
Semolina	1 cup
Fresh coriander, chopped	1 tbsp
Garlic	2 cloves
Bishops weed	1 tsp
Red chillie powder	1 tsp
Turmeric powder	½ tsp
Salt to taste	

Method

Wash and chop the tomatoes into big pieces. Purée in a liquidiser with the skins. The fibre content of the skin is valuable to us for roughage. Add the garlic and half the chick pea flour and blend well. Add the balance chick pea flour and blend once more. Finally add the semolina, Bishops weed, chillie powder, turmeric powder and blend till everything is thoroughly mixed. If you are not immediately preparing the omelettes, refrigerate the batter in an airtight container. It will stay good for up to a week.

The omelettes are prepared like thick dosas. Drop one ladleful of batter on a hot griddle and spread it around in a circular motion using the back of the ladle. Lower the flame. If the griddle is too hot the omelette will burn without being cooked properly. When the colour of the omelette changes to a pale red and the edges lift easily, turn over and cook the other side. Make medium-sized omelettes or they could break while turning over since only semolina has been added. Rice flour, which is used in the conventional recipe of the tomato omelette, binds the batter better but you may be adding calories without adding proportionate fibre or nutrition.

Serve piping hot with the mandatory green chutney and tomato ketchup.

Serves 4-6

Onion-Dal Pakodas

Who does not feel like a little bit of fried snacking once in a way? These pakodas could fool you. While they are easy on your stomach they also give fortified nutrition. And they are not fried.

Ingredients

Bengal gram	½ cup
Mung dal	½ cup
Rice flour	1 tbsp
Chickpea flour	1 tbsp
Onions, finely chopped	4 medium
Chillie powder	1½ tsp
Or to taste	
Green chillie, deseeded and chopped fine	1
Pepper powder	½ tsp
Coriander leaves, chopped fine	1 tbsp
Asafoetida	¼ tsp
Salt to taste	

Method

Wash and soak the dals for an hour. Grind with as little water as possible. Transfer to a big bowl and add the chopped onion. Then add the rice flour, chick pea flour, green chillies, red chillie powder, pepper powder, chopped coriander and salt, to make a thick batter to fashion pakodas out of. If the batter is too runny add extra chick pea flour. Shape into flat round pakodas.

Pre-heat the oven to 250°C. Grease a biscuit sheet and place the pakodas on it. Smear lightly with oil. Bake at 220°C for 20 minutes or till done.

Serve hot with tomato sauce or mint chutney.

Idlis with Sprouts

A value added idli that looks more attractive for it. I was a little concerned about it's reception but it has become quite popular with the family.

Ingredients

Uncooked rice or idli rava	3 cups
Black gram	2 cups
Mung bean sprouts	1 cup
Red bean sprouts	1 cup
Salt to taste	

Method

Wash the rice and black gram and soak separately for an hour. Grind the black gram to a paste. Leave the rice/rava slightly coarse. Mix the two together in a bigger vessel, add salt and mix again. Leave to ferment for 14–16 hours.

Prepare idlis in an idli cooker or a pressure cooker without putting the weight on. Grease the idli moulds lightly and fill them three-fourths with batter. Sprinkle a tablespoon of the sprouts on each idli. Steam for 15–20 minutes.

Serve hot with wet or dry chutney and sambhar.

Opposite: Idlis with Sprouts

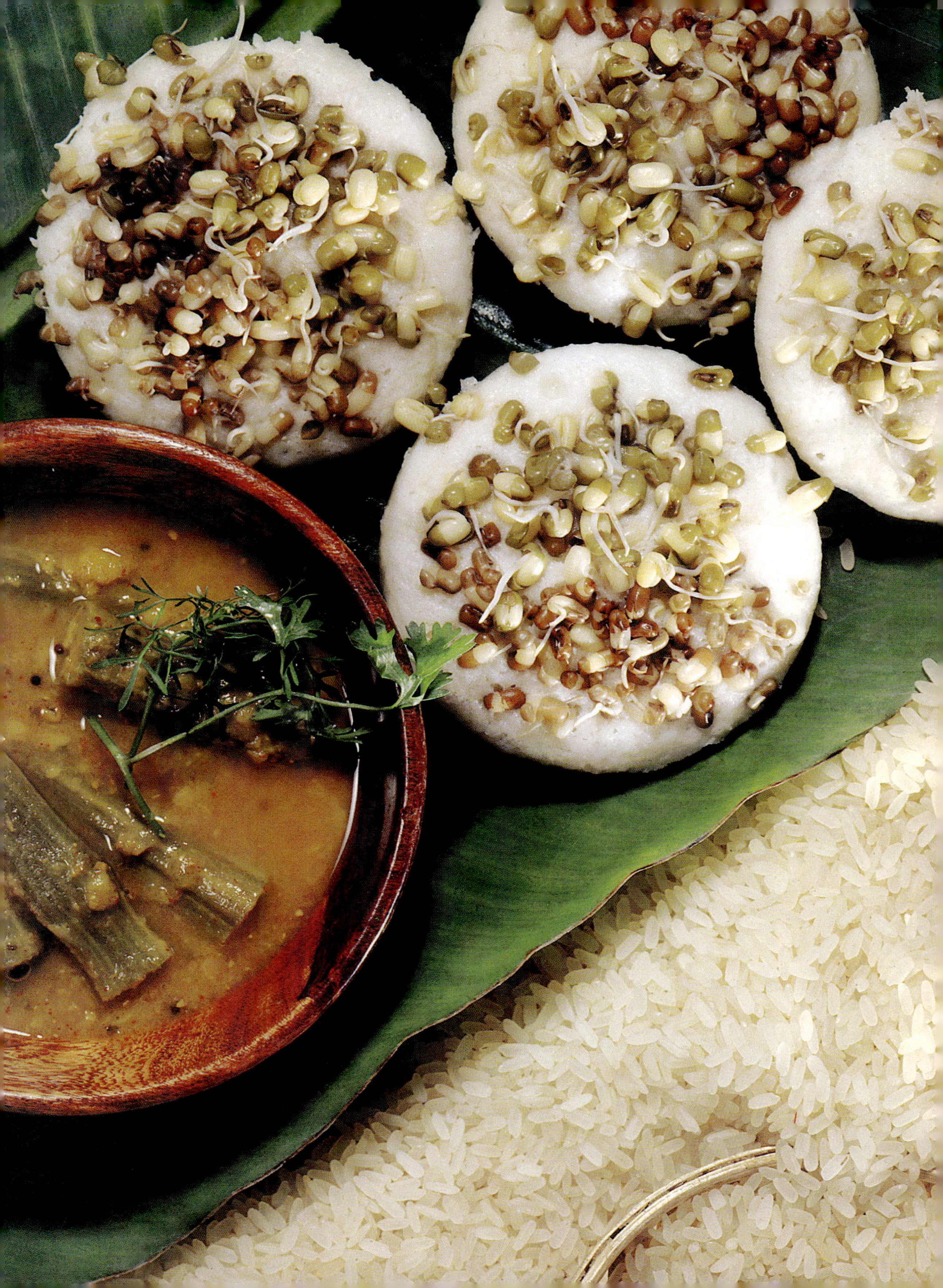

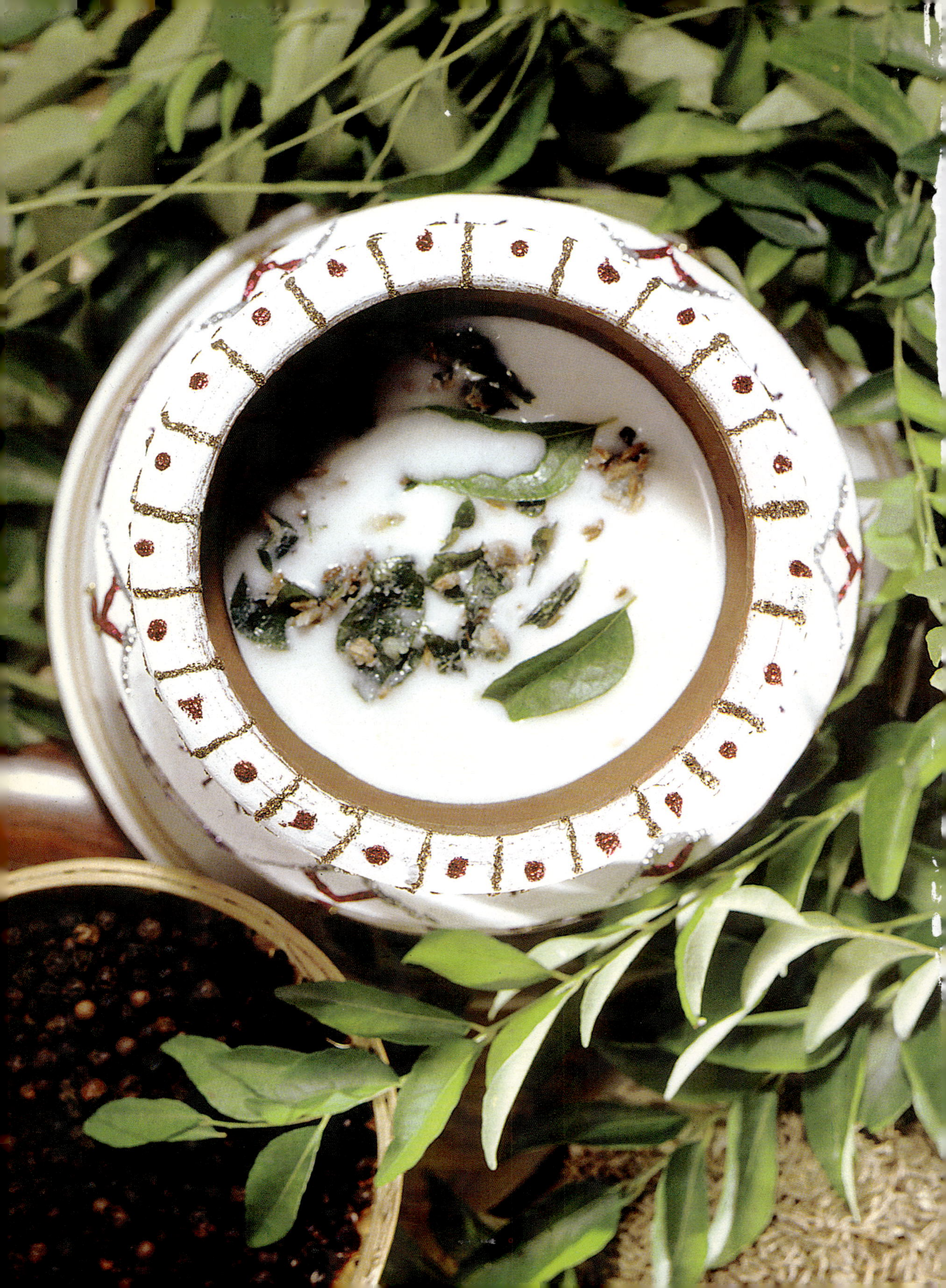

Serves 4-6

Brown is Beautiful

These idlis too are no-rice idlis but they have another great ingredient and that's rye flour. They look a little unconventional and have great curiosity value. They taste so good that you'll definitely put them on your menu once a fortnight at least.

Ingredients

Semolina	2 cups
Rye flour	2 cups
Sour yogurt	1 cup
Ginger, chopped fine	1 tbsp
Green chillies, deseeded, chopped fine	2
Black pepper, crushed	1 tsp
Salt to taste	

Method

Beat the yogurt and mix in the semolina and rye flour. Add salt and adequate water to make a batter as in any other idli (i.e thick dropping consistency). Leave to ferment overnight.

Add the ginger, pepper and chillies just before preparing and mix lightly. Grease the idli moulds and fill them with the batter. These idlis will not rise as much as the conventional idlis. Steam for 15-20 minutes. After taking them out of the cooker leave for a couple of minutes before scooping them out with a spoon.

Serve hot with a green chutney.

Opposite: The Cool One (ref. page 133)

The No-Rice Idli

Serves 4-6

These idlis are light as air and extremely tasty. They are also recommended for diabetics and others who have to eliminate rice from their diet. But it gives a whole lot of assimilable proteins instead.

Ingredients

Mung dal	1 cup
Black gram	1 cup
Salt to taste	

For the Seasoning

Oil of your choice	1 tbsp
Mustard seeds	1 tsp
Curry leaves	8–10
Dry ginger powder or	1 tsp
Fresh ginger, chopped fine	1 tbsp
Pepper, crushed coarsely	1 tbsp
Osr to taste	
Turmeric powder	½ tsp
Asafoetida	¼ tsp
Chopped cashew nuts (optional)	2 tbsp

Method

Wash and soak the two dals separately for an hour. Grind each to a fine paste using some of the water that they have been soaked in. Do not add excessive water. Mix the two batters in a bigger vessel that gives this upwardly mobile batter space to rise. Add salt to taste and beat well to mix thoroughly and leave to ferment for 14–16 hours. Do not beat the batter before putting into the idli moulds or else the idlis could fall flat.

Heat oil in a frying pan and put in the mustard seeds. When they splutter add the cashew nuts and the rest of the seasoning ingredients. Mix the seasoning into the batter. Do not mix vigorously. Grease the idli moulds lightly and fill them three-fourths with the batter.

Heat adequate water in an idli cooker or pressure cooker and place the moulds in it. Steam for 15–20 minutes. Take out of the cooker and leave for a couple of minutes before you scoop them out with a spoon. They turn out extremely light, so handle them with a light hand.

Serve hot with coconut chutney and dry powder.

Soy Khaman Dhokla

Soybean is low in carbohydrate and high in fibre and protein. It is therefore recommended for diabetics too. Soybean is rich in lecithin, calcium and iron. It is very high in polyunsaturates and contains no cholesterol. What more can we say in favour of the soy dhokla?

Ingredients

Gram dal	1 cup
Soy beans	¼ cup
Plain yogurt	1 cup
Green chillies	6
Ginger, chopped	2 tbsp
Instant yeast	2 tsp
Lime juice	2 tbsp
Salt to taste	2 tbsp
Oil of your choice	2 tbsp

For the Seasoning

Oil of your choice	2 tsp
Mustard seeds	1 tsp
Coconut, grated	2 tbsp
Sesame seeds	2 tbsp
Fresh coriander, chopped fine	1 cup
Green chillies, deseeded, chopped fine	1 tbsp

Method

Wash and soak the gram dal and soy beans separately in plenty of water overnight. The next morning wash and drain, then grind in a mixer with green chillies, ginger, yogurt and warm water, to make a thick paste. Add four tablespoons soy oil and salt. Keep the paste in a warm place to ferment for at least 5–6 hours.

Boil water in a large pan or pressure cooker. Grease a small cake pan. In a bowl place two teaspoons lemon juice and yeast. Pour three teaspoons of warm water on this and mix till the yeast dissolves. Then mix in the paste quickly and thoroughly. Then pour into the greased pan. Steam for 10 minutes or until khaman dhokla is done. Remove from steam and leave for two minutes. Cut into squares. Heat 2 teaspoons oil in a small pan, add mustard seeds and asafoetida. Stir-fry for a few seconds, add sesame seeds, coconut and chopped green chillies, and sauté for a few seconds. Garnish dhoklas with seasoning and coriander leaves. Serve with green dhania chutney.

Serves 4-6

DIP, DIP, DIP CHUTNEYS, RAITAS ...AND SAUCES

For the benefit of all those of us who care about what goes into our mouths, it's not the bread that's fattening it's what is spread on it. While you can eat the flat breads with a curry or a salad, you need to have something wet and juicy on your moulded breads. The easiest to reach out to is dairy butter. You might like to know that 100 gms butter has a total of 81 gms fat of which 54 gms is saturated (the kind that raises your cholesterol levels) and 20 gm is monounsaturated and 3 gms is polyunsaturated. Some of us have started opting for margarine in the belief that we are opting for fewer saturated fats – 36 gm– but bear in mind that it has a concentration of 9–14 gm of trans fats which settle down as arterial placque over a period of time. Currently, in most parts of the world, sunflower or safflower margarine is available and this seems to be the better alternative.

This margarine has the highest vitamin E content and only 16 gms saturated fat. The trans fats content ranges from 0.4 to 7gms per 100 gms. Certainly it is not a sin to spread a generous dab of homemade butter occasionally but the best substitute to a bread spread seems to be olive oil – cold pressed extra virgin at that. Even a jot of sesame oil will give the same flavour. There are a few low-fat breads available internationally but these are high in salt content and have more than 60 per cent water.

So the best bet are the chutneys, dips and spreads that follow here – rich in fibre, natural sugar and nutrients specific to each ingredient retained in as natural a form as possible. Better still these can be made in advance and stored for long. They are just what you need in your busy life.

Tomato-Date Sandwich Spread

There's no sugar added and yet it has a natural touch of sweetness. This one takes the prize for minimum no of ingredients that constitute a tasty spread.

Ingredients

Tomatoes, chopped	6 medium
Dates, deseeded	2 cups
Red chillie powder Or to taste	1 tsp
Oil	1 tsp
Rock salt to taste	

Method

Grind the tomatoes and the dates together in the blenderiser. Heat the oil in a thick-bottomed pan and pour the mixture into it. The oil is only to prevent the mixture from burning. Add the salt and the chillie powder and cook till it thickens to a jam-like consistency. Stir occasionally to make sure that it does not burn. Leave to cool and store in an airtight jar in the refrigerator.

Serves 4-6

Ash Gourd Skin Chutney

Fresh coconut is the most common denominator in Indian chutneys but here the ash gourd skin offers the same creamy, fibrous flavour, thereby cutting down on the coconut proportion. Once you taste this chutney, you'll end up buying ash gourd just for the peels!

Ingredients

Chopped ash gourd peels	2 cups
Sesame	2 tsp
Grated coconut,	½ cup
Green chilies, chopped	3-4
Tamarind	2 inch piece
Salt to taste	
Mustard seeds	1½ tsp
Fenugreek seeds	¼ tsp
Turmeric powder	½ tsp
Asafoetida	¼ tsp
Oil of your choice	2 tsp

Method

Heat the oil in a pan and place the mustard seeds in it. When the seeds start to splutter put in the fenugreek seeds, green chillies, sesame seeds and the turmeric and asafoetida. Then add the chopped ash gourd peels and stir-fry for about 5 minutes, adding a little water if required. Finally add the coconut and stir-fry till it is nicely browned. Leave to cool.

Add the salt and tamarind and adequate water for grinding the chutney and blend in the blenderiser. Use as a spread on bread, rotis, parathas or even idlis and dosas.

Serves 4-6

Yellow Pumpkin Chutney

We use only the soft centre portion of the yellow pumpkin which you would otherwise discard. But it adds a nice smooth texture to the chutney and a mildly sweet flavour.

Ingredients

Chopped yellow pumpkin pulp	2 cups
Bengal gram dal	1 cup
Black gram dal	1 tbsp
Dry red chillies	4-5
Tamarind	2 inch piece
Mustard seeds	1½ tsp
Turmeric powder	½ tsp
Asafoetida	½ tsp
Salt to taste	
Oil of your choice	2 tsp

Method

Dry roast the Bengal gram and black gram together till you get a roasted aroma and the dals have lightly browned. Leave to cool.

Heat the oil in a pan and place the mustard seeds in it. When they splutter add the red chillies and the turmeric and asafoetida. Then put in the pumpkin pulp and stir-fry for 5 minutes. Add a little water if needed. Leave to cool.

Blend in a liquidiser, the roasted dals first. When that is powdered add the pumpkin and the tamarind and salt together to make the chutney. Serve with rice or dosas or use even as a sandwich spread.

Mint – Coriander Chutney

This is literally, the evergreen chutney. It has been a hot favourite through all the culinary fashions and is also very versatile. It keeps well and makes a great picnic hamper ingredient along with wafer thin cucumber slices and wholemeal bread.

Ingredients

Chopped mint	1 cup
Chopped coriander	1 cup
Ginger	1 inch piece
Green chillies	2–3
Tamarind	2 inch piece
Rock salt and sea salt to taste	

Method

Clean and wash the mint and coriander thoroughly before chopping them. Then blend the whole lot of ingredients together in the blenderiser. That's all there is to this tantalising hot and sour chutney.

Serves 4-6

Date - Tamarind Chutney

This is actually meetha chutney in camouflage. By making it thick it doubles in utility. Serve with parathas, sandwiches or make roti frankies using this as a spread with cheese. Great idea?

Ingredients

Dates, deseeded	1 cup
Tamarind	2 lemon-sized balls
Cumin seeds	1 tsp
Ginger	1 inch piece
Red chillie powder	1 tsp
Rock salt or sea salt	½ tsp

Method

Grind all the ingredients together in the blenderiser to form a fine paste. Stays for up to a month if well refrigerated.

Serves 4-6

Cabbage Dal Chutney

A good idea when you feel like going on a raw vegetable binge. Have it with plain steamed rice and you'll appreciate the simpler things in life.

Ingredients

Cabbage chopped	3 cups
Grated coconut	¾ cup
Bengal gram dal	1 cup
Black gram dal	1 tbsp
Red gram dal	1 tsp
Sesame seeds	1 tsp
Dry red chillies	3-4
Mustard seeds	1 tsp
Turmeric powder	½ tsp
Asafoetida	½ tsp

Method

Clean but do not wash the dals. If you wish you can rub the dals in a kitchen towel to rid them of any coating. Dry roast the dals in a pan till they turn a golden brown and spread a lovely aroma in your kitchen. Leave to cool.

Heat the oil in a pan and put in the mustard. When it splutters add the red chillies and stir-fry for a minute. Then add the turmeric and asafoetida and take off the flame.

Pick out the red chillies from the seasoning and add them to the roasted dals. Grind the dals, cabbage and the coconut to a coarse paste. Add the salt and blend once more. Transfer to a serving bowl and mix in the seasoning.

Brinjal Chutney

This chutney has all the ingredients of the baingan bharta, except the yogurt. This chutney is an irreplaceable item on picnics. Simply because it makes a great sandwich spread. In the Middle East you get ready to eat rotis called khoubs, something similar to our naans, only they are much softer. The brinjal chutney makes a great stuffing for the khoubs.

Ingredients

Brinjal, roasted	1 large
Onion, chopped	1 medium
Tomatoes, chopped	2 medium
Garlic	1 clove
Green chillies, chopped	2-3
Ginger	1 inch piece
Cumin seeds	1 tsp
Mustard seeds	½ tsp
Turmeric powder	½ tsp
Asafoetida	¼ tsp
Oil of your choice	2 tsp
Salt to taste	

Method

Roast the brinjal as you do for the bharta. Leave to cool and peel off the skin. Chop the tomatoes and scoop out the soft centre flesh which contains water. You can use this in a gravy or soup. But if you leave it in it will make the chutney runny and thereby make the sandwiches soggy. Alternatively, stir-fry the tomatoes along with the onions so that the moisture evaporates.

Heat the oil in a pan and place the mustard in it. When the mustard splutters put in the cumin seeds and asafoetida and turmeric powders. Then add the onion and stir-fry till the onion turns translucent.

Blend the brinjal, onion, tomatoes, green chillies and ginger in the blenderiser. You will not need to add any water. This also makes a great dip for tacos or tortillas.

Serves 4-6

Clusterbeans Chutney

You have some leftover gavar and don't know what to do with it? Here's help. Next time you'll buy extra gavar just to make this chutney.

Ingredients

Chopped cluster beans	3 cups
Raw groundnuts	1 cup
Sesame seeds	1 tsp
Green chillies	4-5
Mustard seeds	1 tsp
Asafoetida	½ tsp
Turmeric powder	½ tsp
Oil of your choice	2 tsp
Tamarind	3 inch piece
Salt to taste	

Method

Clean, wash and top and tail the beans. Heat the oil in a pan and put in the mustard seeds. When they start to splutter put in the asafoetida and turmeric powders and then add the cluster beans. Stir-fry for a couple of minutes and add the groundnuts and green chillies. Stir-fry for five minutes more till the beans are slightly cooked, add a little water, if necessary. The idea is not to cook the beans as you do in the curries. They should be just softened yet retain their bright green colour and at the same time become easy to digest. Leave to cool.

Add the tamarind and salt and blend in the blenderiser to make a fine paste. Add the minimum amount of water required to blend. Serve with rice or rotis, as sandwich spread or a dip.

Note: This dip makes a great conversation opener because no one will ever guess what went into it !

Soyabean Chutney

A good way to fortify a meal. It takes a little time to get used to the strong flavour of soya but build it into your menu and you won't notice it after a while.

Ingredients

Soya beans, soaked overnight	¼ cup
Chopped fresh coriander	1 cup
Green chilies	5–6
Ginger, chopped	2 inch piece
Lime juice	5 tbsp
Salt to taste	

For the Seasoning

Soy or any other oil of your choice	1 tsp
Mustard seeds	1 tsp
Curry leaves	5–6
Asafoetida	¼ tsp

Method

Cook the soya beans in boiling water for about 10 minutes. Leave to cool. Add the other chutney ingredients and blend into a paste with a little water.

Prepare the seasoning by heating the oil in a pan and adding the mustard seeds to it. When the seeds begin to splutter add the curry leaves and asafoetida and sauté for a minute. Mix the seasoning into the chutney and serve with idlis, dosa or use as a spread for sandwiches.

Serves 4-6

Tofu – Mint Dip

Serve with everything from tortillas and parathas to crackers and frankies. Makes a great taste substitute for eggs and meat.

Ingredients

Chopped fresh mint	3 cups
Tofu	½ cup
Green chillies	3–4
Ginger, chopped	2 inch piece
Cumin seeds	1 tsp
Lime, juiced	1 large
Salt to taste	

Method

Blend all the ingredients in the blender until the mixture becomes a smooth paste.

Transfer to a glass jar and refrigerate till required.

Serves 4-6

Mango Onion Preserve

This seasonal preserve is a must-make, must-have, for it tangy flavour. Serves as a spread for sandwiches, rotis or even with a biryani.

Ingredients

Grated green mango	2 cups
Grated onion	1 cup
Red chillie powder	2 tsp
Sugar to taste	2 tsp
Salt to taste	

For the Seasoning

Oil	1 tsp
Cumin seeds	1 tsp
Fenugreek seeds	4-5
Turmeric powder	½ tsp
Asafoetida	¼ tsp

Method

Heat oil in a thick-bottomed pan. Place the cumin seeds in it. When they start to move around add the rest of the seasoning ingredients and stir-fry for 30 seconds. Then add the rest of the ingredients and cook till it becomes well blended and of a spreading consistency. Take off the flame and leave to cool. Store in an airtight glass jar in the refrigerator.

Serves 4-6

Nutty About Nuts

Here is food that gives you an instant mood lift. Make your own peanut butter at home. It turns out to be a great sandwich spread but can be used to fortify rotis too.

Ingredients

Raw peanuts	1 cup
Roasted split chick peas	1 tbsp
Red chillie powder	1 tbsp
Or to taste	
Tamarind	1 inch piece
Salt to taste	
Oil of your choice	1 tsp

Method

Blend all the ingredients, except the oil in a blenderiser. The whole thing will turn into a lump because of the oil content in the nuts. Then add the oil and blend once more to a spreading consistency.

Gun Powder

No self-respecting South Indian will have his/her idli/dosa without this ammunition on the side. It has a nice grainy, crunchy texture to it because it is ground coarse, not fine. The authentic way to eat it is by mixing it in a small amount of sesame oil. But I have discovered that it tastes just as nice with olive oil.

Ingredients

Blackgram dal	½ cup
Dry red chillies	1 cup
Or to taste	
Bengal gram	½ cup
Fenugreek seeds	1 tsp
A pinch of asafoetida	
Salt to taste	
Oil	1 tsp

Method

Heat the oil in a pan and roast the red chillies till they turn crisp. Then dry roast the 2 dals separately. You can add fenugreek seeds to either one of them halfway through the roasting since they require very slight warming up. Then add the rest of the ingredients and grind them in the dry grinder without adding any water. This powder will keep well for up to a month even if stored at room temperature.

DALS AND OTHER ACCOMPANIMENTS

If you are a vegetarian or are planning to be one, your main concern is going to be how to fulfil your requirement of protein. For all this while you have believed that animal meat has been taking care of this major nutritive requirement. The truth is that the human body does not imbibe protein directly through the protein it consumes. The protein must first be digested and split into its component amino acids. The body can then use these amino acids to construct the protein it needs. What we need therefore is foods rich in amino acids. Plants can synthesize amino acids but animals and humans are dependent on plants. There are 20 different amino acids that the body needs. Of these, 12 are produced by the body and eight must be assimilated through the food we eat.

In a vegetarian diet soybean is the most complete vegetable protein. Grains, legumes, seeds, nuts and vegetables are all rich in the eight essential amino acids but most do not contain all eight of them. Therefore it is necessary to have a varied vegetarian diet. You can combine grains with legumes as in dal and rice, or peanut butter and chapatti; adding vegetables also helps supply additional proteins as in sambhars – vegetables; dairy and grains as in kadhi – yogurt with ragi flour. This is something the Indian cook has been doing through the ages. But often becoming aware of it's importance opens up possibilities of creating better food combinations. And here follow a few ideas...

Kadhi Lajawaab

Serves 4-6

Dairy products contain a high quality of protein. Making sure that they are low fat will not only prune the unnecessary calories but also increase assimilation of the nutrients. Combine them with a grain like ragi or millet and you have a rich source of protein and calcium. That's what this kadhi is all about.

Ingredients

Ragi flour	3 tbsp
Sour curds or plain	1 cup
Mung sprouts	¾ cup
Oil for seasoning	
Red chilly powder	1 tsp
Asafoetida	½ tsp
Turmeric powder	½ tsp
Grated ginger	1 tbsp
Curry leaves	4–5
Salt to taste	

Note: You can substitute ragi with bajra flour.

Method

Beat the yogurt well and mix in the ragi flour. Add about 5 cups water, mix well and set aside. Heat oil in a thick-bottomed pan and place the mustard in it. When it splutters add the asafoetida, cumin, turmeric and stir-fry. Add the curry leaves and ginger and fry for 30 seconds. Add the ragi flour in yogurt mixture and stir well. Add the red chillie powder and let it cook for about 5 minutes. Do not cover the pan or the liquid will boil over. Ragi takes a little longer than chick pea flour to cook, so stir occasionally and let it cook till it starts to thicken. Add more water if required and then add the mung sprouts and salt. Cook for a couple of minutes more and take off flame. Garnish with fresh coriander and serve hot with either rice or rotis. This kadhi tastes better on the hotter side.

Spinach with Lentils

Another tasty way to increase your consumption of proteins – combining vegetables with a legume. Make sure you add an extra large dose of vitamin C – plain lime juice – to the dal, in order to help assimilation of the iron content in the spinach or palak.

Ingredients

Palak	1 bunch
Mung beans, split cooked	4 cups
Coconut, grated, optional	1 tbsp
Lime, juiced	1 big
Salt to taste	

For the Seasoning

Oil of your choice	1 tsp
Cumin seeds	1 tsp
Turmeric powder	½ tsp
Asafoetida	¼ tsp
Fenugreek seeds	¼ tsp
Ginger, chopped fine	2 inch piece
Whole pepper	1 tsp
Green chillie, slit lengthwise	1

Method

Clean and wash the palak thoroughly and chop it. Set aside. Clean and wash and cook the mung beans. Set aside.

Then prepare a seasoning with the seasoning ingredients. Heat the oil in a pan and place the cumin in it. When it starts to move around add the turmeric and asafoetida and stir-fry for a few seconds. Add the rest of the ingredients and stir-fry for a minute. The green chillie is slit and not chopped so that it is not mistaken for the spinach when cooked.

Add the chopped spinach to the seasoning and stir-fry for a minute. Add adequate water and cook till almost done. Then add the cooked mung beans, coconut and salt and mix well. Cook till the palak is done. If you add salt during the cooking process the nutrients get leached, therefore add the salt towards the end. This may not be possible in the case of certain vegetables but being aware of this will help. Take off flame and transfer to a serving dish. Add the lime juice just before serving. Serve hot with plain steamed rice and don't forget the papad!

Bottle Gourd with Split Yellow Mung

Serves 4-6

A south-Indian favourite, this goes well particularly with rice. But since both the bottle gourd and mung dal have a bland creamy taste, spiking it with a generous quantity of lime juice is mandatory.

Ingredients

Bottle gourd, skinned and diced	500 gm
Yellow Mung cooked	3 cups
Coconut, grated, optional	1 tbsp
Tomato, cubed	1
Lime, juiced	1
Fresh coriander, chopped for garnish	1 tbsp

For the Seasoning

Mustard seeds	½ tsp
Cumin	1 tsp
Ginger, chopped fine	2 inch piece
Whole pepper	1 tsp
Green chilly, slit length-wise	1
Curry leaves	5-6
Fenugreek seeds	¼ tsp
Oil of your choice	1 tsp

Method

Cook the split yellow mung partially. Set aside Prepare the seasoning by first heating oil in a pan and placing the mustard seeds in it. When they begin to splutter add the cumin and turmeric and asafoetida powders. Stir-fry for half a minute and add the rest of the seasoning ingredients and stir-fry for a minute.

Then add the diced bottle gourd. Add to this about three cups of water and cook till almost done. Then add the cooked dal, salt to taste and cook till the gourd is thoroughly done. Mix well and spike with lime juice just before serving. Transfer to a serving dish and garnish with the chopped coriander.

Note: A bouquet garni of coriander and curry leaf stalks will add to the aroma and nutrition of the dal.

Serves 4-6

The Cool One

This one is ideal for the hot summers, the curry leaves help purify blood. It's a no-cook recipe, so no sweating over the stove.

Ingredients

Tender curry leaves	1 cup
Coconut, grated (optional)	½ cup
Whole peppercorns	8–10
Buttermilk	3 cups
Salt to taste	

For the Seasoning

Ghee	½ tsp
Cumin seeds	1 tsp
Turmeric powder	½ tsp
Asafoetida	¼ tsp

Method

Wash the curry leaves and pat them dry. Blend the curry leaves, peppercorns and coconut to a fine paste in the blenderiser. Then add the buttermilk and salt and blend these too. Transfer the cool kadhi to a serving bowl. Prepare a seasoning by heating the ghee in a pan. Place the cumin seeds in it. When they start to move around add the rest of the seasoning ingredients and stir fry for 30 seconds. Pour the seasoning over the kadhi and chill if desired. Serve with porridge, rice, or even as an appetiser.

Note There are other ingredients which can be substituted for curry leaves in preparing this kadhi. Here is a list of substitutes and the roles they play:

Neem: kills infections/Holy basil: antidote for cough and cold/Tender leaves of lime tree: improve appetite/Tender leaves of drumstick tree: purify blood and cure skin problems/Lemon grass leaves: antidote for fevers/Coriander: increases body fluid and counteracts respiratory problems/Tender fenugreek leaves: cures arthritis and piles/Tender leaves of tamarind tree: antidote for excessive bile/Tender linseed leaves: cures congestion and excessive bile

Ash Gourd Sambhar

Another South Indian staple which goes well with rice and is invariably served at festive meals. The ash gourd neutralises all the other spicy pungent food.

Ingredients

Ash gourd, skinned	500 gms
Red gram dal, cooked	4 cups
Coconut, grated	1 tbsp
Sambhar masala	3 tbsp
Tamarind	1 lemon-sized ball
Coriander stalks	5–6
Fresh coriander, chopped	1 tbsp

For the Seasoning

Oil	2 tsp
Mustard seeds	1 tsp
Fenugreek seeds	¼ tsp
Cumin seeds	½ tsp
Curry leaves	5–6
Turmeric powder	½ tsp
Asafoetida	¼ tsp

Method

Cook the dal till soft and set aside. Skin the ash gourd and preserve skins for use in chutney. Chop off the soft portion of the ash gourd and reserve for use in soups. Chop the rest of the gourd into 1 inch cubes. Soak the tamarind in a cup of water and extract the juice. In a deep thick-bottomed pan place the ash gourd cubes and pour the tamarind extract over it. Add enough water to cover the vegetable and cook it. Tie up the coriander stalks together and float them into the mixture. Add the sambhar masala and just enough salt required for the vegetable and cook till the ash gourd becomes soft but not squishy. By this time your neighbours would have come over to ask what's cooking because the aroma of the sambhar masala would have invited them in.

Next, mash the cooked dal thoroughly so that it has no identity of its own and add it to the vegetable. Again add salt, now for the sake of the dal. If you add all the salt right at the beginning the vegetable will absorb it all and taste like the salt pans of Mumbai. The cooked dal will also contain some amount of water but if you wish you could add more water to bring the sambhar to the consistency you desire. Bring the mixture to the boil, let it simmer for five minutes and take off flame.

Heat the oil in a pan and place the mustard seeds in it. When they splutter add the rest of the seasoning ingredients, stir-fry for a minute and pour the seasoning directly on to the sambhar. This is probably the high point of the cooking when the aroma of the seasoning infuses with the aroma of the cooked sambhar. Inhale deeply. Cover the sambhar immediately so that the aromas infuse together.

Just before serving pick out the coriander stalks, sprinkle the chopped coriander on top and serve hot with rice, idli, dosa.

Note: You can substitute ash gourd for almost any vegetable like drumstick, pumpkin, ladies finger, broad beans, cluster beans, onions. Baby onions or Madras onions taste great but whatever vegetable you use make sure that the pieces are big or else they will get lost in the cooking.

Serves 4-6

Blackgram Sprouts

When you sprout a seed it is transformed into a tiny easily digested plant brimming with amino acids in complete protein form, vitamins and easily assimilated minerals.

Ingredients

Black gram sprouts	4 cups
Onions, peeled and sliced	2 medium
Tomatoes, quartered	2
Ginger, peeled and chopped	2 inch piece
Green chillie, chopped	1
Garlic, peeled	6-8 colves
Red chillie powder	1 tsp
Cumin seeds	1 heaped tsp
Turmeric powder	½ tsp
Coriander powder	1 tbsp
Cumin powder	½ tbsp
Garam masala	½ tsp
Fresh coriander, chopped	1 tbsp
Plain yogurt, beaten	1 cup
Oil	2 tsp
Salt	to taste

Method

Clean and wash the whole black gram thoroughly. Soak it for about 12 hours in lots of water. Change the water as often as you can (at least twice in 12 hours), since the protein in the gram starts giving off an odour when it breaks up into monocorts and dicorts. Then drain off the water and tie the gram up in a clean muslin cloth or use sprout makers (easily available in the market). It will take another 24 hours for it to sprout.

Meanwhile wash the gram gently or just hold them in a colander under running water. In the beginning it seems like a lot of effort but once you get into a routine you'll stop noticing it. It is a good idea to sprout all whole grams in this way since we gain a lot more of their nutrition when they sprout and also so that they are easier on the digestion.

We all know the not so silent announcements we make when we consume whole chick peas and black gram! Sprouts are one good way to avoid flatulence. Once the sprouts are ready you can store them in the refrigerator up to a week.

To get back to our recipe – cook the black gram for about 10-15 minutes till it is soft. Leave to cool.

Meanwhile prepare a paste of onion, garlic, ginger, tomato and green chillie. Heat the oil in a thick-bottomed pan and place the cumin in it. When the cumin starts to move add the turmeric powder and stir-fry for 30 seconds. Then add the freshly ground paste and sauté till it turns brown and stops giving off a raw smell. Mash the gram with the spatula and mix in the rest of the ingredients, except the coriander, ginger juliennes and yogurt. Cook the gram till the masalas are well-blended. Take off flame and keep covered.

Just before serving mix in the yogurt, reserving a tablespoon to decorate in a swirl on the top. Sprinkle the chopped coriander and ginger juliennes around it and serve hot with rotis or rice. It is a filling and fulfilling dish in terms of nutrition and taste.

Whole Chick Peas in Tamarind Sauce

Cooked tomatoes turn acidic and create discomfort. It is therefore a good idea to substitute tomatoes as a souring agent with tamarind. Sprout the whole chick peas in the same manner as whole black gram.

Ingredients

Whole chick peas	4 cups
Tamarind soaked in 2 cups water	1 cup
Onions	2 medium
Ginger	2 inch piece
Green chillie	1
Red chillie powder	1 tsp
Coriander powder	1 tbsp
Cumin powder	½ tbsp
Turmeric powder	1 tsp
Garam masala	¼ tsp
Cumin seeds	1 tsp
Oil	2 tsp
Salt to taste	

Method

Cook the whole chick pea sprouts with adequate water for 10–15 minutes till they turn soft. Leave to cool. Meanwhile grind the onion, ginger, garlic and green chillie to a paste. Extract tamarind juice from the soaked tamarind.

Heat the oil in a thick-bottomed pan and place the cumin seeds in it. When they begin to move add the turmeric powder and sauté for 30 seconds. Add the onion paste and sauté till it turns light brown. Then add the tamarind extract to it and the cooked chick peas. Finally add the rest of the ingredients, except the chopped coriander and the ginger juliennes. Do not forget to add the salt at this stage. Cook till everything is well-blended and of the right consistency. If required add a little water.

Garnish with the chopped coriander and ginger juliennes and serve with rotis, rice or even a loaf of bread. This makes an excellent brunch too.

Serves 4-6

Fenugreek-Millet Special

Another great grain-vegetable combination to fortify ourselves with the requisite amino-acids. Traditionally it is made with chick pea flour but substituting it with millet has the extra advantage of a grain that has maximum alkaline reaction among the grain group.

Ingredients

Fenugreek leaves	1 bunch
Millet flour	1 cup
Green chilies, chopped	2
Mustard seeds	1 tsp
Turmeric powder	¾ tsp
Asafoetida	½ tsp
Oil	2 tsp
Salt to taste	
Green chillie, slit lengthwise	1
Onion, finely sliced	1 small

Method

Clean and wash the fenugreek thoroughly. Chop coarsely. Heat the oil in a thick-bottomed pan and place the mustard seeds in it. When they splutter add the turmeric, asafoetida and green chillies and sauté for 10 seconds. Then add the fenugreek leaves and enough water to cook. Cook covered for about five minutes. Then sprinkle the millet flour with one hand while mixing in the fenugreek with the other hand, to prevent the formation of lumps. Add salt and required water to let the flour cook thoroughly. Cook covered, stirring occasionally till the mixture thickens and the flour is cooked. Transfer to a serving dish.

Garnish with the slit green chillie and sliced onion and serve hot with rotis or phulkas.

ONE-DISH MEALS

If necessity is the mother of invention, one-dish meals belong to her family tree. You'll see why – if you are a working mother you need to spend quality time with your kids whatever their ages or gender. If you are a stay-at-home mother you are virtually the CEO of the household and you end up spending time fixing everybody elses' routines. If you are single you need to fend for yourself. If you are a couple living on your own, you want to optimise your time in the kitchen so that it can be channelised elsewhere.

If you are creative in your cooking you will want to see how well you can blend taste and nourishment within the time crunch. If you just eat to live, then all you look for is the recommended daily requirement in a given number of calories. So it seems that whoever you are and whatever you do, the one-dish meal is an idea whose time has come. Here are several such ideas that minimise on time and optimise on nutrition. Take your pick.

It's Different! Ven Pongal

This is a traditional dish from the state of Tamil Nadu state in India, made with rice and yellow lentils. In spite of being a rice dish, it puts in a regular appearance on breakfast menus. Here we have substituted rice with broken Bulgar wheat. The creamy texture of lentils combined with the milky wheat taste makes this as good as the original. Though of course, it's different.

Ingredients

Bulgar broken wheat	2 cups
Lentil	1 cup
Salt to taste	

For the Seasoning

Cumin seeds	2 tsp
Ginger	1 inch piece
Curry leaves	5–6
Whole peppercorns	1 tsp
Ghee	2 tsp
Turmeric powder	¼ tsp
Asafoetida	¼ tsp

Note: Bulgar broken wheat grain are the size of broken basmati. If this is not available you can use any coarsely ground dalia or lapsi semolina.

Method

Clean, wash and soak the broken wheat for 20 minutes. Clean, wash and drain the lentils.

Heat the ghee in a pan and place the cumin seeds in it. When the cumin begins to move add the rest of the seasoning ingredients and sauté for 10 seconds. Reduce the flame and sauté the broken wheat and lentils till all the grains are coated with the seasoning. Add seven cups of water and cook till almost done. Then add salt and mash well. If there is excess water cook for a couple of minutes more while stirring continuously to prevent burning.

This is a khichree that has the consistency of a thick porridge. If desired you may add an extra dollop of ghee for garnish and serve piping hot.

Serve with roasted papad and methkut saar.

Serves 4-6

Spinach - Broken Wheat Khichree

Fibre in the wheat and folic acid in the spinach are a great combo for a balanced meal. Serves well for diabetics too.

Ingredients

Spinach	1 bunch
Bulgar broken wheat	2 cups
Onion, diced	1 medium
Ginger, minced	2 inch piece
Garlic cloves, minced	2
Amchur	½ tsp
Anardana	¼ tsp
Oil of your choice	1 tbsp
Fresh coriander, chopped for garnish	1 tbsp

Whole Masala

Bay leaf	1
Cloves	4
Pepper corn	1 tsp
Cardamom, split	1 big

Method

Clean, wash and chop the spinach. Clean, wash and drain the Bulgar wheat.

Heat the oil in a pan and add the whole masalas. Sauté for 30 seconds till you get a rich aroma. Then add the onions and sauté till they turn translucent. Add ginger and garlic and sauté for 10 seconds more. Then add the broken wheat and sauté till it is well-coated with oil. Finally add the chopped spinach and add five cups of water to this and the salt. Cover the pan and cook till soft. Mash well and transfer to a serving bowl. Garnish with chopped coriander.

Serve hot with kadhi and a crisp salad to set off the mushy khichree.

Fistful of Great Taste – Muthiya

They get their name from the way they are made; by taking a fistful of dough. The variation here is that we use only wheat semolina instead of the heavy-to-digest chick pea and wheat flour combination. This steamed dish can even be offered as convalescent food since it is steamed and is also rich in fibre.

Ingredients

Cabbage, shredded fine	500 gms
Semolina	2½ cups
Green chillies	3
Ginger	2 inch piece
Asafoetida	¼ tsp
Oil of your choice	1 tbsp
Salt to taste	
Fresh coconut, grated (optional)	2 tbsp
Fresh coriander, chopped	1 tbsp
Lime, juiced	1

Opposite: Muthiya

Method

Put the semolina in a large bowl and make a well with your finger, in the centre. Mix the oil with salt and leave to sit for five minutes. Make a paste of the ginger and green chillies.

Add the salt, ginger-chilly paste, asafoetida and knead well into the semolina. Finally add the cabbage and knead again. The cabbage has enough moisture to bind the semolina so do not add any water to make the dough. Make small rolls by pressing the dough between your fingers and palm.

Lightly grease two pans and place the rolls in them. Steam the rolls for 15–20 minutes. Check whether they are done by inserting a toothpick. If it comes clean take the steamer off the flame. Transfer to a serving plate and drizzle the lime on them. Toss well to coat evenly. Garnish with the grated coconut and chopped coriander.

Serve hot with a red hot coconut-garlic chutney and a mulligatawny soup.

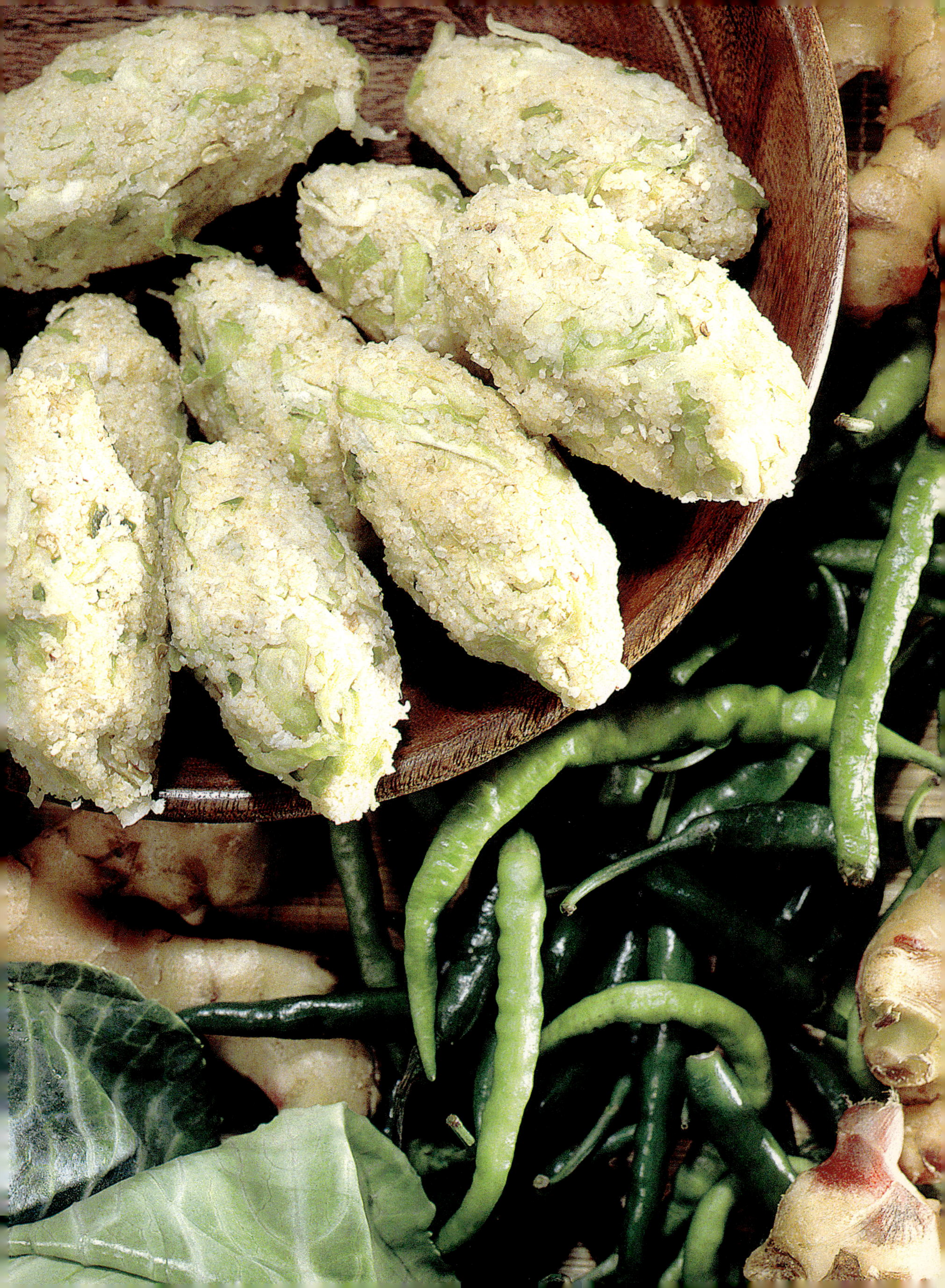

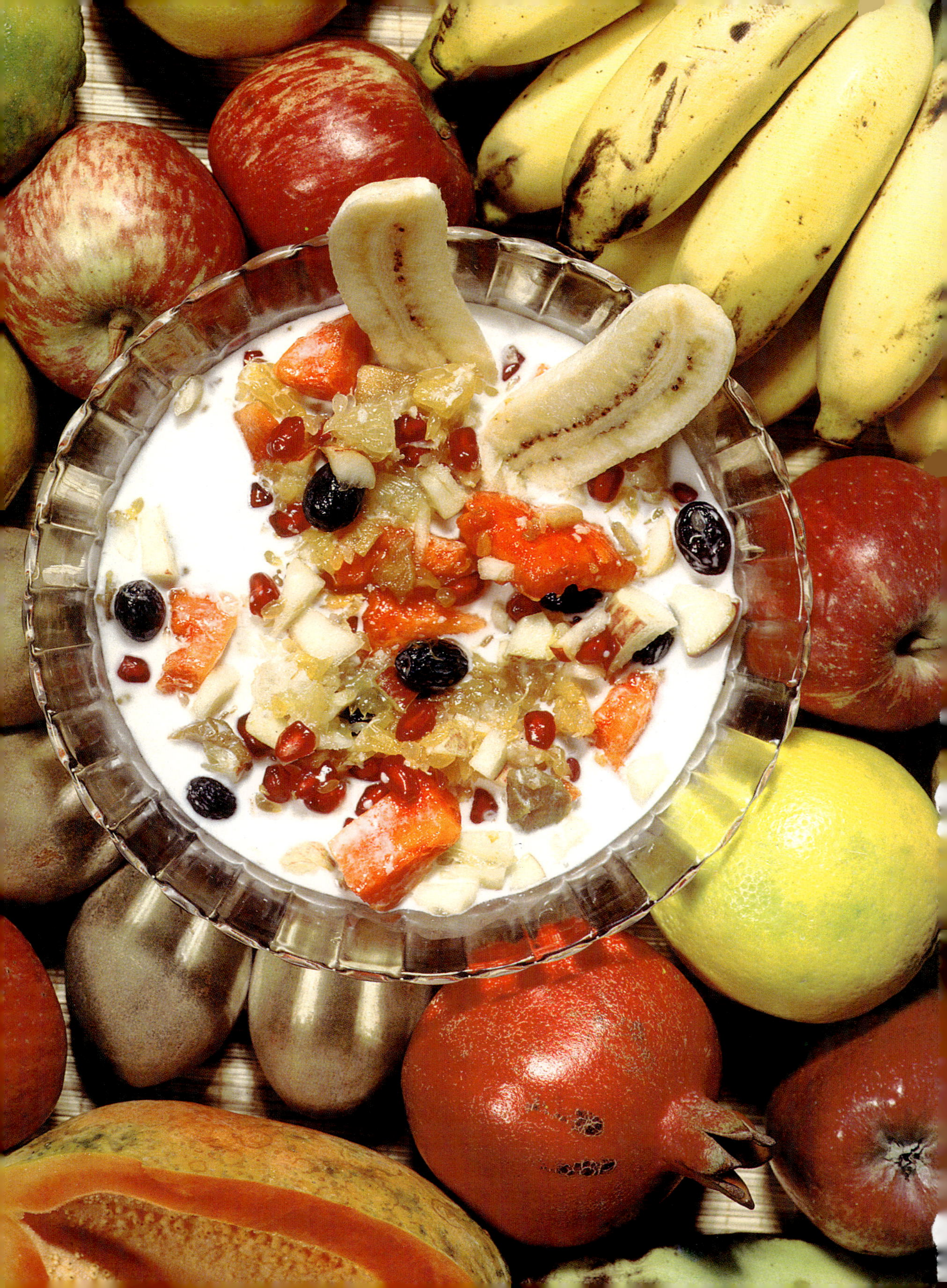

Millet Khichree

Millet being a highly alkaline grain, it can be consumed as often as possible. The common way to use it is in breads but millet semolina can be used to make a khichree too.

Ingredients

Millet semolina	1 cup
Split yellow lentils with skins	1 cup
Fresh coconut, grated (optional)	1 cup
Salt to taste	

For the Seasoning

Cumin	2 tsp
Turmeric powder	1 tsp
Asafoetida	½ tsp
Curry leaves	5–6
Ghee	2 tsp
Fresh coriander, chopped fine for garnish	1 tbsp

Method

Prepare the semolina by dry roasting the millet and grinding in a dry grinder or coffee mill. The semolina must be of coarse texture, not fine. But perhaps you are lucky enough to get your friendly neighbourhood flour mill to do this for you. Clean, wash and drain the yellow lentils with skins. Heat the ghee in a pan and place the cumin seeds in it. When they begin to move add the rest of the seasoning ingredients and sauté for 10 seconds. Add the washed lentils to this and sauté till you get a rich aroma. Then add the millet semolina and coconut and six cups of water and cook for 10 minutes or till soft.

Mash well and transfer to a serving bowl. Garnish with the chopped coriander and serve hot with methkut saar.

Opposite: Honey – Fruit Cornpote (ref. page 155)

Dal Dhokli

Such a clever way to combine a meal you will not find elsewhere. You only have to add a salad by the side and a smart meal is ready and waiting. Only don't let it wait too long or else the dhoklis will turn into their original form (dough) again. A bit of a Cinderella effect here.

Ingredients

For the Dhokli

Whole wheat flour	4 cups
Millet flour	¼ cup
Celery seeds	1 tsp
Turmeric powder	1 tsp
Oil	2 tsp
Salt to taste	

For the Dal

Split red lentil	1½ cups
Onion, chopped fine	1 medium
Garlic cloves, minced	2
Ginger, minced	1 inch piece
Green chilies, chopped fine	2
Salt to taste	
Lime, juiced	1
Fresh coriander, chopped fine	2 tbsp

For the Seasoning

Fenugreek seeds	5–6
Mustard seeds	1 tsp
Cumin seeds	½ tsp
Turmeric powder	1 tsp
Asafoetida	½ tsp
Curry leaves	5–6
Oil	2 tsp

Method

Clean, wash and cook the red lentil with lots of water till soft. Set aside. Prepare a thick dough by kneading well all the dhokli ingredients together, using adequate water. Roll out big size rotis, slightly thicker than normal and cut into one inch diamonds/squares to make the dhoklis. Repeat process until the entire dough is used up. Spread the dhoklis on kitchen paper till all are made.

Heat oil in a deep thick-bottomed pan and place the mustard in it. When it splutters add the rest of the seasoning ingredients and sauté for 10 seconds. Then add the onion, garlic and ginger and sauté till they turn translucent. Mash the cooked lentil and add to the seasoning. Add salt, dry mango powder and the anardana. Bring to a boil and drop the dhoklis in one by one. Bring to a boil and then simmer for 15–20 minutes till the dhoklis are well-cooked. Stir occasionally to prevent sticking and add extra water to the dal if you feel it is becoming lumpy. The dhoklis must have enough space to move around. Take off heat and mix in the lime juice. Transfer to a serving bowl and garnish with coriander.

Serves 4-6

Some Like it Hot

This porridge is made with a mixture of rye and millet flours, in equal proportion - available at general stores or could be ground at your friendly neighbourhood flour mill. Since it is made with sour yogurt, it has a nice tangy taste to it. The fresh ginger and pepper add to the bite. It is better to have it hot with a dab of butter, either homemade or clarified, since it congeals on cooling.

Ingredients

Pepper, freshly crushed	1 tsp
Fresh coriander	1 tbsp
Rye flour	1 cup
Millet flour	1 cup
Sour yogurt	2 cups
Fresh ginger, chopped fine	1 tbsp
Green chillie, chopped fine	1
Freshly grated coconut	1 cup
Water	6 cups
Salt to taste	
Clarified butter	2 tsp

For the Seasoning

Mustard	1 tsp
Turmeric powder	½ tsp
Asafoetida	1 tsp
A few curry leaves	
Oil	2 tsps

Method

Heat the oil in a thick-bottomed pan and place the mustard in it. When it splutters add the turmeric and the other seasoning ingredients. Stir-fry for 30 seconds. Then add the water slowly. When the water comes to a boil, lower the flame and add the rye flour with one hand while stirring continuously with the other. Then add the millet flour while stirring continuously. When the entire flour is added, mix thoroughly and add the coconut and yogurt. Mix thoroughly again. Then add the salt. Let it cook on a low flame for about 10 minutes, while stirring occasionally to prevent sticking. The mixture should have the consistency of porridge. When the mixture starts leaving the sides of the vessel, the porridge is cooked. Add the ghee, take off the flame and keep covered for five minutes.

Serve hot with lime pickle and a dab of butter.

Serves 4-6

Pasta in Dill Sauce

Who doesn't love variety? It's amazing what a few familiar ingredients could do to an unfamiliar one- create a unique taste. Don't pass this by, try it.

Ingredients

Dill, chopped	1 cup
Spring onions, chopped	1 cup
Garlic cloves, minced	2
Eggplants, diced	4 medium
Tomatoes, diced	2 big
Pepper	1 tsp
Corn flour	1 tbsp
Mozarella cheese Or	50 gm
Tofu Or	50 gm
double the quantity of arrowroot flour	
Extra virgin olive oil	2 tbsp
Rock salt to taste	
Sea salt to taste	
Plain spaghetti	500 gm

Method

Prepare spaghetti as per instructions on the packet, drain and set aside. Heat one tablespoon olive oil in a big thick-bottomed pan. Stir in corn flour and mix well. Add one cup of water and mix well. Add the chopped dill and crumble in the mozarella cheese and cook covered for two minutes. Add another cup of water and cook covered till the sauce turns thick. If you choose not to use the cheese, substitute with tofu or double the quantity of arrowroot flour.

In another thick-bottomed pan place the onion and garlic along with the remaining tablespoon of olive oil. Stir-fry for a couple of minutes, add the eggplant cubes and the tomatoes and stir-fry for two more minutes. Then add the rock salt, sea salt and pepper and enough water to cook the vegetables. Cook covered. Turn off the flame in approximately five minutes, when the vegetables turn tender and chunky but not mashed. Add these vegetables to the dill sauce and mix well. Check and adjust seasoning. The final sauce must be of thick pouring consistency.

Serve the spaghetti in individual plates and pour the hot sauce on top. A basket of garlic bread looks and tastes great with this dish.

Serves 4-6

Pasta in Spinach Soya Sauce

This is a traditional recipe with minor changes that add to the goodness value of the pasta.

Ingredients

Spinach, chopped fine	2 cups
Soya milk powder	3 tbsp
Corn flour	1 tbsp
Extra virgin olive oil	1 tbsp
Spring onions, sliced fine breadthwise	1 cup
Garlic, minced	2 cloves
Pepper powder	1 tsp
Rock and sea salt to taste	
Macaroni	500 gms

Note: The soya milk powder can be substituted with plain low-fat milk.

Method

Prepare the macaroni as per the instructions on the packet, drain and set aside. Mix the soya milk powder in a cup of water and keep ready to add to the sauce.

Heat the olive oil in a thick-bottomed pan and stir in the corn flour. When it is mixed well add a cup of water and mix again. Keep stirring or the sauce can turn lumpy. When the sauce comes to the boil add the seasoning with the prepared soya milk. Stir well and then add the spinach, onion and garlic. Add water if required and cook covered, stirring occasionally, for about five minutes. The sauce must be of thick pouring consistency. Cook covered for a couple of minutes more and turn off flame.

Serve the macaroni on individual plates and pour the sauce on top. A side dish of garlic bread goes well with it.

SINLESS SWEETS — WELL ALMOST

The idea of eating right is not to deprive yourself of the things you enjoy but to modify them to work for you. While we have to make a conscious effort to do this, our ancestors seem to have been quite successful at it. Then came along the industrial revolution and the advent of factory made sugar instead of the manually churned out jaggery or gur. Before that there was honey and of course the high-energy dates.

A judicious mix of these ingredients can lend the same sweetness and make you a healthier person too. While dates and honey contain more calories measure for measure, they also contain easily absorbed glucose, which is a boon to people suffering from low sugar levels. Apart from this they also contain other trace minerals while sugar has empty calories.

Date Dumplings

Serves 4-6

Modaks are traditionally made with a filling of fresh coconut and sugar. Here dates and figs are used instead of the sugar. The figs lend a lovely crunchy texture and the dates give a sweetness without making it cloying. If eating is believing, you should try this.

Ingredients

For the Filling

Coconut, grated	1
Dates, deseeded and puréed	¼ kg
Dried figs, puréed	¼ kg
Chopped cashew nuts and almonds	1 tbsp
Poppy seeds	1 tbsp
Cardamom powder	¼ tsp

For the Covering

Rice flour	3 cups
Water	4 cups
Oil of your choice	1 tsp

Method

For the Filling

Chop the deseeded dates and figs. Blend them along with the grated coconut and poppy seeds in a mixer. Add the chopped nuts and blend once more. In case the mixture turns out a little thin you may have to stir-fry with a little ghee in a thick-bottomed pan, till it can be shaped into a ball. Shape the entire mixture into lemon sized balls.

For the Covering

Add two drops of oil to the water and bring to a boil. Reduce the flame and slowly add the rice flour while stirring continuously with your other hand. Keep stirring till no lumps are left. Let it cook, stirring continuously, till it forms the consistency of a dough. Take off the flame. Grease your hands with the oil and shape the dough first into lemon-sized balls. Then work the dough only with your thumb and pointer finger to shape into a cup so that the date-coconut ball can fit into it. Pinch together the edges of the cup to seal and twist into a peak shape. This is the modak. Or you can make them as plain round balls too. Grease the inside of the steamer lightly before you place the modaks. You can use a modern steamer or a traditional idli stand for this purpose. Steam the modaks for 15 minutes. Serve hot or cold.

Serves 4-6

Honey Fruit Compote

The Fit for Life diet has wrought some drastic changes in the lifestyles of its loyal followers. Personally I have found that I am much more energetic and comfortable on an all-fruit breakfast. But since combining fruits with milk or ice cream is not recommended, much of the fun of gorging on fruit seems to be sacrificed. This compote is so delicious that it'll make you an instant convert to a fruit breakfast.

Ingredients

Bananas, diced	5
Sweet limes, peeled and diced	2
Oranges, peeled and diced	2
Grapes	100 gms
Apples, diced	2
Pomegranate, peeled and cleaned	1
Fresh coconut grated Or	½
Coconut cream Or	250 ml
Mango juice	250 ml
Honey	¼ cup
Jaggery, grated Or chopped fine (optional)	1 tbsp
Lime, juiced	1

Method

Chop the bananas in a bowl and pour the lime juice immediately over it to prevent the bananas from discolouring. Set aside a tablespoon of pomegranate and add the rest to the bowl. Then add the rest of the fruits and the grated coconut or coconut cream. Mix well. Add the grated jaggery and mix again. Finally add the honey and mix well together so that the flavours get well blended. Transfer to a glass serving bowl because you will want to show off the attractive multi-coloured compote. Garnish with the pomegranate you have set aside. Chill for not more than 15 minutes. Serve in individual bowls. Be prepared for demands for second and third helpings!

Brownies (Hayagreev)

Sometimes one looks forward to festivals mainly for the food that comes with them. In fact, let me be honest and say, most of the time. Hayagreev is one such festive sweet that brings back fond memories and is always accompanied by an encore. Traditionally this is made with split chickpeas or chana dal. Since chana dal is heavy to digest, here we have substituted it with mung dal.

Ingredients

Mung dal	1 cup
Grated jaggery	1 cup
Grated fresh coconut	1 tbsp
Poppy seeds	1 tsp
Chopped almonds and cashew nuts	1 tbsp
Kismis or sultanas	10–12
Cardamom powder	¼ tsp
Finely sliced pista	1 tbsp

Method

Soak the mung dal for 10–15 minutes and pressure cook for 10 minutes. In a heavy-bottomed pan mix together the cooked dal, grated jaggery, poppy seeds, chopped nuts and sultanas and place on a low flame. Make sure you stir occasionally or else the mixture will get burnt. Cook till it reaches a semi-dry consistency. Just before taking it off the flame, mix the cardamom powder into the mixture and keep covered for 5 minutes.

Grease a small cup with ghee and make moulds of the hayagreev to serve as brownies. Or you can just spoon out the mixture, garnish with sliced pista and serve.

Serves 4-6

Steamed Brownies

Sometimes a little bit of fancy covering makes it that much more of a value added item. Particularly if the value is both in terms of taste and nourishment.

Ingredients

Mung dal	1 cup
Grated jaggery	1 cup
Grated fresh coconut	1 tbsp
Poppy seeds	1 tsp
Finely chopped almonds and cashew nuts	1 tbsp
Kismis or sultanas	10–12
Cardamom powder	¼ tsp

For the Covering

Rye flour	1 cup
Water	2 cups
Oil of your choice	1 tsp

Method

Soak the mung dal for 10–15 minutes and pressure cook for 10 minutes. In a heavy-bottomed pan mix together the cooked dal, grated jaggery, poppy seeds, chopped nuts and sultanas and place on a low flame. Make sure you stir occasionally or else the mixture will get burnt. Cook till it reaches a semi-dry consistency. Just before taking off the flame mix the cardamom powder into the mixture and keep covered.

Add a couple of drops of oil to the water and bring to a boil. Then add the rye flour, a little at a time and stir continuously till it reaches the consistency of a dough. Take off the flame. Leave to cool for 5 minutes.

Smear your palms and fingertips with a little oil and with a small portion of the dough shape a cup using your thumb and pointer finger. Place a teaspoon of the filling in this cup and seal the edges. Roll into a ball again. Steam these brownies in an idli stand or a steamer for 10–15 minutes. Serve hot with a pat of homemade butter.

Chocolate Fudge

Serves 4-6

Soya provides us more proteins at a cost of fewer calories than even lean meat. At the same time it is more easily digestible. You can't find another synonym more appropriate for health food. Therefore we've used Soya milk instead of dairy milk here. Honey is the preferred sweetener! So here goes.

Ingredients

Soya milk, fresh or prepared from powder	300 ml
Cocoa	30 gms
Homemade butter or sunflower margarine	55 gms
Honey	1 cup
Crushed walnut	1 cup
Liquid glucose	1 tbsp
Cream of tartar	A pinch

Method

Combine all the ingredients together in a thick-bottomed pan and cook on a medium flame till the mixture starts leaving the sides of the pan. Take off the flame and stir till the mixture cools. This is the conventional fudge consistency but if you wish to cut it into cubes then keep on the flame for just a couple of minutes more. Transfer to a storage container if you are planning to store it or to a glass dish if you are serving soon. This is best kept refrigerated though it is doubtful that it will last long enough to worry about!

Sevai

Serves 4-6

Traditionally prepared by the Muslims as a festive sweet, a tiny change in the ingredients adds to the goodness value.

Ingredients

Durum vermicelli	2 cups
Finely sliced jaggery	2 cups
Ghee	1 tsp
Pistachios	2 tbsp
Saffron strands	½ tsp
Water	6 cups

Note: The jaggery gives you fortified calories and traces of iron while Durum wheat contains fibre.

Method

If the vermicelli is not already broken, break it into small bits. Melt the ghee in a thick-bottomed pan and put in the vermicelli. Lower the flame and stir-fry the vermicelli till it turns a golden brown and imparts a delicious aroma.

Add the water to the roasted vermicelli and when it comes to a boil put in the jaggery. Stir occasionally to make sure that the jaggery does not burn. When the jaggery has melted cover the pan and cook for 10 minutes, stirring occasionally.

When the vermicelli is soft and cooked, turn off the flame. If there is excess water cook uncovered for a few minutes, while stirring occasionally. Crush the saffron in a tablespoon of warm water with the back of a spoon and mix it with the cooked vermicelli. (Make sure that you stir gently or you could end up with vermicelli mash.) Transfer to a serving dish. Garnish with the chopped pistachios. Serve hot or chilled.

Date Pancakes

Serves 4-6

If you've drooled over Chinese date pancakes and regretted it because they're dripping with fat, here's some good news. Try these, they're slimmer and tastier.

Ingredients

For the Filling

Dates	½ kg
Grated or desiccated fresh coconut	1 cup

For the Pancakes

Durum semolina	1 cup
Wholemeal wheat flour	2 cups
Oil of your choice	2 tbsp
Rice flour	½ cup

Method

Mix the semolina and the wheat flour in a largish vessel. Add 1 tablespoon of the oil to it and knead well. Add adequate water to make a dough. Then add a little more water (about a tablespoon at a time) and knead some more till the dough attains an elastic consistency. You could do this in an electric dough maker and save yourself a lot of effort. Add the rest of the oil and set aside the dough till you get the filling ready.

Deseed the dates and blend them along with the coconut. Since dates are a sticky affair, literally speaking, it's better to do them in small installments. When the whole lot has been puréed set aside.

Take a portion of the dough, the size of a small lime and with your thumb and pointer finger greased lightly, fashion a cup. Put in one and a half teaspoon of the filling and pinch together the edges to seal. Roll into a ball between your palms and flatten. Roll it out like you do a paratha about six inches in diameter. Roast on both sides on a hot griddle without using any shortening.

Pan roasted date pancakes turn out crisp and yummy. They taste good even when cold. Serve as a tea-time snack with a tangy dip or even as part of a meal.

Simply Tempting

Some of us don't have a sweet tooth, we have a sweet cavity where our stomach should be. This carrot halwa is meant for just such people. You can eat it by the cupful without worrying too much because we have substituted the khoya, burnt milk with soya milk. More proteins, calcium and fewer calories.

Ingredients

Grated Indian winter carrots	4 cups
Sliced jaggery	2 cups
Chopped dates	10-12
Raisins	1 tbsp
Soya milk, fresh or prepared	2 cups
Ghee	1 tbsp
Chopped almonds	1 tbsp
Cardamom powder	1 tsp
Saffron strands	¼ tsp

Method

Put the milk in a thick bottomed pan and add the grated carrot to it. Cook uncovered, stirring continuously, till almost all the milk has been absorbed. Then add the jaggery and continue stirring. When the jaggery melts, the mixture will turn a darker shade of pink. Then add the chopped dates and raisins. Crush the saffron in a tablespoon of hot water and add this to the boiling mixture. When the mixture thickens and leaves the sides of the pan take off the flame. Mix in the cardamom powder and keep covered for 5 minutes so that the cardamom essence is infused in the mixture. Transfer to a serving dish and garnish with chopped almonds. Serve hot or chilled. It can serve as a dessert or as an accompaniment to rotis.

Makes 5-6

Yummy Rolls

This sweet has its antecedents in the Middle East. There it is made with condensed milk. But you will find that a judicious mix of dates with dry fruits will eliminate the need for condensed milk altogether. Need I add that this will outsell even the legendary hot cakes.

Ingredients

Almonds, blanched, skinned and powdered	1 cup
Walnuts, powdered	1 cup
Cashew nuts, powdered	1 cup
Pistachios, powdered	1 cup
Raisins, puréed	1 cup
Dates, puréed	1 cup
Desiccated coconut	1 cup

You will need plastic cling film

Method

Immerse the almonds in hot water for 10 minutes and then skin. Let them dry off for a couple of hours. Any moisture retained at this stage could lead to a drastic reduction in the staying power of the rolls. When the almonds are thoroughly dry, powder them in a blender in small batches as nuts secrete oil, and tend to stick together. The same goes for the rest of the ingredients as well. Take brief breaks so the blender motor does not overheat. Mix the entire lot of powders and purées in a large vessel so that the tastes and flavours blend with each other. Then using both your palms shape oblong rolls that measure about 4–5 inches and are about 2 inches in diameter. Spread the desiccated coconut on a clean surface and coat the rolls. This gives them a shop-made finish that is as attractive as the taste itself. But rememeber the coconut is entirely optional and if you wish you can skip this step. Then wrap each individual dry-fruit roll in cling film and store in an air-tight container. These rolls will stay for up to a year if you freeze them. Unwrap them and cut into roundels of desired thickness before serving.

Serves 4-6

Temptation

This is another sweet fit for the gods and coveted earnestly by us mortals. The sweet taste of coconut milk fused with the essence of cardamom and the aroma of roasted pulses makes this irresistible. In this matter simply follow Oscar Wilde's advice: 'The only way to treat temptation is to give in'.

Ingredients

Yellow (mung) dal, roasted	1 cup
Split chick peas, roasted	¾ cup
Sliced jaggery	1½ cups
Almonds, blanched	1 tbsp
Raisins	1 tbsp
Pistachios, sliced for garnish	1 tbsp
Cardamom	¼ tsp
Coconut cream, first extract	1 cup
Coconut cream, second extract	2 cups
Saffron strands	¼ tsp

Method

Roast the dals together till they turn a golden brown and impart a strong aroma. Wash them well and soak in 4 cups water for 15 minutes. Grind the almonds to a paste and set aside. Cook the dals for 10–15 minutes. They should turn to mash on pressing lightly. The chick peas will, however, remain a little crunchy even after cooking. Mash the dals in the vessel with the back of a thick spoon.

In a thick-bottomed vessel put in the second extract coconut cream and mix in the almond paste. Add the raisins and heat on a low flame till it comes to a boil and then add the mashed dals. Mix well and continue stirring so that the bottom does not burn. When this mixture comes to a boil add the first extract coconut cream. Before it comes to a boil again add the sliced jaggery and turn off the flame. Continue stirring till the jaggery melts. Take a teaspoon of the hot coconut milk and crush the saffron strands in it with the back of a spoon. Put this back into the pudding. Then add the cardamom powder and keep covered for 5 minutes.

Serve hot or chilled in individual cups, garnished with the sliced pistachios.

Carrot Almond Pudding

This is the most delicious way to eat carrots. What a treat to the eyes and the tastebuds this gorgeous pudding can be!

Ingredients

Carrots	500 gms
Soya milk or cow's milk	1 ltr
Almonds	½ cup
Cardamom, crushed	1 tsp
Jaggery, sliced	400 gms

Method

Cook the carrots with just enough water. Leave to cool. Meanwhile, if you are using Soya milk prepare it. In a thick bottomed deep pan bring the milk to a boil and simmer it to let it thicken. Blanche the almonds and grind half the quantity to a paste. Then add the cooked carrots and grind together in a liquidiser. Add this to the simmering milk and stir well to prevent burning. Turn off the flame after a couple of minutes and add the jaggery. Stir well till it dissolves in the heat of the pudding. Add the cardamom powder, stir well and keep covered for 5 minutes to let the aroma infuse into the pudding. Take lid off the pan and leave to cool to room temperature and then chill the pudding or kheer for an hour in the refrigerator. Cut the rest of the blanched almonds into slivers.

Serve the kheer in individual bowls and garnish with the almond slivers.

Serves 4-6

Sweet Potato Delight

This recipe won an award for my mother on her first foray into competitive cooking ages ago. It is amazing how well balanced it is in the nutritive values and the correct process of cooking them. It's a family heirloom and I would love to share this with you.

Ingredients

Sweet potatoes	300 gms
Soya milk or cow's milk	1 ltr
Jaggery	1 cup
Ghee	1 tsp
Crushed cardamom	1 tsp
Almond or pista slivers for garnish	1 tbsp

Method

Wash the sweet potatoes thoroughly and scrape off the skin wherever dirty. Chop it once lengthwise and then slice into slightly thick roundels. Heat the ghee in a deep thick-bottomed pan and sauté the roundels till they turn pink. Add the milk to the pan and bring it to a boil. Lower the flame and let the milk simmer. Stir the mixture occasionally so that it does not stick or burn. When the sweet potato roundels are cooked and the milk has thickened, turn off the flame. Add the jaggery and stir till it dissolves. Then add the cardamom and keep covered for five minutes.

Serve into individual bowls and garnish with pista or almond slivers. This will be a chunky type of kheer and the aroma is so tempting that you may not want to leave it to chill. Tastes good hot or chilled.

Bottle Gourd Pudding

This is a comeback of the humble bottle gourd as a fabulous dessert. It lends itself beautifully to this creamy sweet taste.

Ingredients

Skinned and grated bottle gourd	400 gms
Prepared Soya milk or cow's milk	6 cups
Blanched and powdered almonds	1 tbsp
Sliced jaggery	1 cup
Crushed cardamom	¼ tsp
Ghee	1 tsp
Sliced pista	1 tbsp
Basil	1 sprig

Method

Heat the ghee in a deep pan and stir-fry the bottle gourd till the kitchen is redolent with a sweet aroma. Pour in the milk and the almond powder and let it simmer till it thickens. Stir occasionally to prevent burning and a curdled texture. Take it off the flame and add the sliced jaggery and stir till it dissolves well. Add the cardamom and keep covered for 5 minutes. Transfer to a serving bowl and garnish with the basil sprig in the centre and sliced pista surrounding it. Leave to cool to room temperature.

Serve chilled.

Whole Wheat Flour Cookies

Easy to make and easy on the stomach – says it all for these cookies. Everyone needs a few of them at tea time or anytime.

Ingredients

Whole wheat flour	250 gms
Deseeded dates	250 gms
Ghee	4 tsp
Cardamom	¼ tsp

Method

Blend the dates in a blenderiser without adding any water. Then add this to the wheat flour in small quantities, along with the ghee and blend it in. An electric hand mixer will do the job fine. Finally add the cardamom powder and blend together again. Shape into small balls and flatten to biscuits between your palms. Heat a griddle, lower the flame and bake these cookies without smearing any oil or ghee on the surface. Bake with the griddle covered with a metal lid. Or simply oven bake them at 200° C for 20 mins or till done. Leave to cool and store in an airtight jar. Or perhaps your family will help in stowing them away in their stomachs!

SPICE-IT-UP MASALAS

Spice is what brings variety to life and here are various ways to add spice to your cooking. But what exactly are spices? Exotic plant extracts no doubt. It is difficult to give a precise definition because each definition leaves out a few spices as we know them. Suffice it to say that spices are the dried parts of aromatic plants – seeds, flowers, leaves, barks or root– although a few are used fresh. The use of spices is not limited to culinary or medicinal alone. They are used to manufacture incense, perfumes, oils, cosmetics, preservatives and flavourings.

As in most good things in life there is a temptation to go overboard with spices. But that would have the exact opposite effect – serving to smother the other ingredients rather than enhance them.

It can also adversely affect your health since each of these spices is a potent drug in its own way.

The best way to prepare a bouquet of spices is to roast spices on a very low flame and just long enough for the aroma to fill the kitchen. Leave to cool for a couple of minutes and dry grind immediately. Leave the powder to cool completely and then store at room temperature in air-tight glass jars. It is best to grind masalas required for a couple of months so that their aroma and freshness is retained. In an ideal world, of course, you would not grind for more than the day's requirement. Aah can you smell them already? Well, let's go make them then.

Goda Masala

Can be used in a variety of curries or prepared rice varieties, amtis and dals.

Ingredients

Coriander seeds	500 gms
Desiccated coconut or grated copra	1 cup
Sesame	100 gms
Asafoetida	1 tsp
Cumin seeds	100 gms
Cloves	1 tsp
Cinnamon	2 inch pieces
Oil	1 tsp

Method

Dry roast the coconut on a low flame. Dry roast the sesame too, separately, on a low flame.

Then roast the rest of the ingredients, except the asafoetida, in oil. Transfer these to a plate and in the same pan sauté the asafoetida.

Grind together the whole lot in the dry grinder to a fine powder. Leave to cool and store in an air-tight jar.

Garam Masala

This is a must-add spice in north-Indian cooking. Just a small pinch will do the job wonderfully.

Ingredients	
Pepper	1½ tbsp
Cloves	1 tbsp
Cumin	1 tbsp
Mace	¾ tbsp
Cardamom pods	¾ tbsp
Bay leaf	1
Cinnamon, broken to bits	1 tbsp

Method

Dry roast the ingredients till you get a mild aroma. Grind together to a fine powder. Cool and store in an air-tight jar.

Coriander Powder

Coriander or dhania has a sweet citrus-like taste and can be used in curries, parathas or dal preparations.

Ingredients	
Coriander seeds	1 cup

Method

Dry roast the coriander seeds on a low flame till you get a mild aroma. Grind to a fine powder in the dry grinder.

Cool and store in an air-tight jar.

Chaat Masala

Adds a zing and a tang to almost any food. Can also be sprinkled on sliced cucumber for sandwiches.

Ingredients	
Cumin seeds	1 tbsp
Whole pepper corn	1 tsp
Red chillie powder	1 tsp
Dry mango powder	1 tsp
Cloves	2
Aniseed	1 tsp
Cinnamon	½ inch piece
Rock salt to taste	

Method

Dry roast all the ingredients except the red chilly and dry mango powders, till you get a mild aroma. Grind to a fine powder in a dry grinder. Then mix in the rest of the ingredients and grind again. This has to be a superfine powder. If you wish you can sieve it to get the right texture.

Cool and store in an air-tight jar.

Cumin Powder

Cumin or jeera powder adds a pungent aromatic taste to peas, gourds and yogurt based curry. Can be used in a dressing too.

Ingredients	
Cumin seeds	1 cup

Method

Dry roast the cumin seeds on a low flame till you get a mild aroma. Grind to a fine powder in the dry grinder. Cool and store in an air-tight jar.

Methkut

Tastes great if mixed with plain steamed rice along with salt, a dash of lime juice and a dab of ghee. There's also a soup recipe given which requires this powder. The inclusion of fenugreek seeds in this makes it a digestive but I would recommend it for its delicate taste and mild flavour.

Ingredients

Bengal gram	1 cup
Rice	½ cup
Split black gram	½ cup
Wheat	2 tsp
Coriander seeds	1 tbsp
Cumin seeds	1 tbsp
Asafoetida	1 tsp
Turmeric powder	1 tsp
Red chillie powder	2 tsp
Mustard seeds	1 tsp
Fenugreek seeds	½ tsp

Method

Dry roast the grams, rice and wheat till you get a rich aroma. Leave to cool and add the rest of the ingredients and dry grind to a fine powder. You can sieve the powder if you wish a really fine texture, which is how it ought to be.

This powder keeps good for a long time.

Sambhar Masala

As the name suggests this masala is used to prepare sambhar but there is no rule that says you cannot use it in innovative ways. You might even come up with a winner.

Ingredients

Coriander seeds	1 cup
Cumin seeds	⅓ cup
Dry red chillies Or to taste	10–15
Red gram	1 tbsp
Split black gram	1 tbsp
Turmeric powder	1 tsp
Asafoetida	½ tsp
Fenugreek seeds	¼ tsp
Mustard seeds	1 tsp

Method

Dry roast the ingredients and grind them fine in a dry grinder. While this masala keeps good for long it is best used when fresh.

TIPS FOR A HEALTHIER LIFESTYLE

✺ Munching is so more-ish isn't it? But you can get sensible about munching. Fill up your coffe-table cookie jars with seeds like sunflower or pumpkin instead of chocolates. Seeds with the skin on are better than the skinned variety. Because the very tedium of shelling will lead you to philosophise the theory of diminishing returns. If you end up consuming a handful of sunflower seeds, it will all be for a good cause — your heart needs the lecithin to clear up the cholesterol clogged up in your arteries.

✺ Two to three portions of fruit are mandatory for good health according to the WHO. While you are at it, have a whole fruit instead of fruit juice. An orange, for example has six times more fibre than a four-ounce glass of orange juice.

✺ To cut down the amounts of fat or oil in your daily cooking, use small amounts of lime juice, orange juice, water, broth or vegetable stock. Okra and aubergine —which you may feel require greater amounts of cooking oil — taste just as great with a squeeze of lime.

Note adding fat substitutes to vegetables in the very beginning may leach the water-soluble nutrients.

✺ Sometimes, modifying the cooking process can itself reduce the amount of fats you use. Stir-fry, is usually a great idea with both vegetarian and non vegetarian food. But when you are in the mood to do without that little bit of oil, boil, simmer, grill, roast, poach, bake or steam. When you want to eat quick-dish warm veggies, instead of the daily salad bowl, just wash, chop and steam them.toss them in a generous dressing of mint coriander chutney and bake for 5-10 minutes.

✺ Looking for a substitute spread for breads? Savour avocado butter. It has zero cholesterol, its full of good fats, and is rich in vitamin E and minerals. And it doesn't take more than five minutes to make — halve an avocado and deseed. Scoop out the flesh and blend with lime juice and garlic, pepper, curry powder or other ingredients of your choice. Transfer to an air-tight jar and refrigerate. But avocado is a high calorie fruit and if you are trying to lose weight, go easy on it.

✺ As a thickener for soups, stews and curries nothing beats millet flour. Millet, or the Indian bajra, is high quality protein, rich in iron, pottasium, calcium and is easily digestable. If you find it difficult to accept a new taste, combine it with the usual cornflour thickener to begin with and then use it on its own. It is easily available at supermarkets and at flour mills.

✸ Soy milk powder is a great substitute for whipped cream in soups. For one, it has zero cholesterol, has more protein and fewer calories. You can even use it in sauces that call for cream or cheese.

✸ Add a couple of tablespoons of bran of any grain — wheat or oats, for instance — to your waffles, pancake or dosa batter.. you will be enriching it with fibre and no one will be the wiser for it.

✸ Barley is recommended for all kidney ailments, it also helps prevent kidney problems. But you can't see yourself guzzling barley water every morning? No problem. Add some extra water to the kettle when you make your morning herbal tea. When the water comes to a boil take what you need for your tea and use the rest to immerse a handful of barley grain. Add this grain to whatever you cook for dinner – soups, dals, curries, stews, rice or sambhar, while cooking. The barley grain is chewy and tasty.

✸ You're late for work again and must take a packed lunch to remain faithful to your health regime? Try this smartwich. Brush some olive oil or any oil of your choice on leftover chapatti, spread a thin layer of any chutney, arrange some slices of cucumber, tomato and sprinkle some cottage cheese or tofu. It will keep you happy till tea-time and lead you on a discovery of new fillings.

✸ You're nuts about peanuts and are always thinking up new ways to get them on your plate? Here's a winner. Add them to any seed you are sprouting. They turn sweeter and milky, not to mention more digestible. When you add these to your salads, believe me, you'll simply want to live on them. They are a great way to stock up on your daily requirement of amino acids.

✸ All this raw food and power lunching is giving you a bloated tummy and sometimes you fear you are going to sound like the Diwali fireworks? Add a liberal sprinkling of Bishops weed, or ajwain, and ginger powder to your salads and cooked food. You'll feel comfortable at all times. This is the best kept secret of the century. So far.

Note: This is an excerpt from an article by the author, that appeared in the Friday Magazine

ACKNOWLEDGEMENTS

Unlike a fiction writer, it is the job of a cookbook author to acknowledge that the inspiration for all the recipes are true life characters. Like your first boss the first cook in your life leaves an indelible impression and this is usually your mother. Mine was a health food cook even before the phrase was coined and this effort is a reiteration of the values handed down from her. Marriage into a family that served food that was different enough from what I was used to to warrant some amount of adjustment, made me rethink the connection between food, health and happiness. I can reassure you the fallout has been positive — many of the recipes have been included here – with a few modifications. And the credit goes to my mother-in-law for her admirable patience in letting me learn from my own mistakes.

A big thank you to my sister-in-law Rajani, for sharing some of her favourite recipes and helping me research others. Also to my friend Neelima, who despite a complicated personal life encouraged me with several tips. And to dear friend Yasmine, for being there when I needed all the help I could get in putting the book together.

This book would literally not have been born if it had not been for the constant support, encouragement and timely nagging of my spouse Ramesh and sons Salil and Sanjit. I shouldn't at all be surprised if they think of the time gone by and wonder how they got through all the experimentation. Their computer savvy helped me greatly in sending the draft through cyberspace and back. My niece and nephew helped happily by making me try harder to please their demanding palates. Not to forget my brother, father and father-in-law who helped by critiquing recipes in cyberspace.

The major influence in understanding the needs of the body was through Dr. H K Bakhru and his pioneering work, simply put through his books and various magazine articles including those written for the publications I worked with. But more than his writing it is his firm faith in his work that sets him apart from bestseller writers riding on a wave to a writer with a message making one. Believe me, he is also the healthiest septuagenarian I have known.

If I had to name one book that started me thinking on some of our ingrained food habits, how they affect us and how we could gain by changing some of them, it would have to be the 'Fit for Life' series by Marilyn and Harvey Diamond.

Last but not the least, I should like to thank my publisher and editor who had faith in me even when I failed to deliver on deadline. May their breed flourish.

INDIAN BOOK SHELF
STAR PUBLISHERS
DISTRIBUTORS
Ph. : (020) 7380 0622
E-mail : indbooks@aol.com
www.starpublic.com

£